The Versatile Vocalist

Singing Authentically in Contrasting Styles and Idioms

Rachel L. Lebon

The Scarecrow Press, Inc.
Lanham, Maryland • Toronto • Oxford
2006

SCARECROW PRESS, INC.

Published in the United States of America
by Scarecrow Press, Inc.
A wholly owned subsidiary of
The Rowman & Littlefield Publishing Group, Inc.
4501 Forbes Boulevard, Suite 200, Lanham, Maryland 20706
www.scarecrowpress.com

PO Box 317
Oxford
OX2 9RU, UK

Copyright © 2006 by Rachel L. Lebon

British Library Cataloguing in Publication Information Available

Library of Congress Cataloging-in-Publication Data

Lebon, Rachel L., 1951–
　　The versatile vocalist : singing authentically in contrasting styles and idioms /
Rachel L. Lebon.
　　　　p.　cm.
　　Includes bibliographical references and index.
　　ISBN-13: 978-0-8108-5741-4 (hardcover : alk. paper)
　　ISBN-13: 978-0-8108-5351-5 (pbk. : alk. paper)
　　ISBN-10: 0-8108-5741-3 (hardcover : alk. paper)
　　ISBN-10: 0-8108-5351-5 (pbk. : alk. paper)
　　1. Singing—Instruction and study.　2. Style, Musical.　3. Performance
practice (Music)　I. Title.
MT820.L43 2006
783—dc22　　　　　　　　　　　　　　　　　　　　　2006001887

∞ ™ The paper used in this publication meets the minimum requirements
of American National Standard for Information Sciences—Permanence of
Paper for Printed Library Materials, ANSI/NISO Z39.48-1992. Manufactured
in the United States of America.

I lovingly dedicate this work to my mother, Georgette Lebon, and in memory of my father, Raymond Joseph Lebon.

Contents

Preface

The art of singing, like all other art forms, is constantly evolving and reflecting our changing world—one in which technology allows us to become influenced globally by diverse cultures and languages, with no boundaries. Our ears and voices are being opened to new sounds and styles, expanding possibilities for vocal expression. As singers explore the myriad ways to communicate emotion and ideas, the professional does not remain static but experiments with different timbres, in different languages, within the traditional and commercial idioms. Ultimately, the ability to be versatile not only opens one to new cultures and perspectives but also enriches the physical, emotional, and intellectual experience of communicating with the human voice.

The conventional wisdom within vocal pedagogy is that the technique of vocal production applies to all vocalism and transcends vocal styles. And it is true that any vocalist whose tone is produced from the throat up, who does not project, lacks resonance, sings at one dynamic level, and is unintelligible is generally not long for the performing world. Ultimately, for singing to be healthy and to project effectively, in both performance idioms and venues, vocal production must emanate from the breath and away from the throat, be resonant with clear enunciation, and remain free from extraneous tensions in the body. But while these constants often transcend style, proprioception (the kinesthetic or sensory feedback that the vocalist senses as he/she is singing) can be quite different. Simply put, what one feels or relates to while singing can and often does contrast sharply in crossing over from one style or idiom to another.

For example, if I sing a soprano aria from an oratorio after having done an extended blues gig on microphone, I must physically reacquaint myself with breathing that will accommodate more sustained phrases (even with coloratura), head resonance, and increased energy for projection (the microphone is no longer assisting!)—not to mention the prosody of another language. The mind is willing, but the flesh is weak. My body initially tries to revert to what is kinesthetically familiar. It can take some time to reorient myself and discard stylistic idiosyncrasies, such as alterations in tongue position or attack, that I might have acquired. What I as an individual relate to tactually can differ from what another vocalist relates to when converting from one idiom to another, complicating the issue in terms of pedagogy.

While the worlds of voice science and vocal pedagogy continue to explore the elements that constitute healthy vocal expression, to my knowledge little has been written discussing the physical adjustments and proprioception inherent in crossing over successfully between contrasting musical idioms. This is particularly true with regard to microphone idioms in combination with instrumental accompaniment. Versatile singer–teachers who have successfully performed within contrasting idioms can draw from their experience in describing the kinesthetic adjustments as they adapt to differing vocal and professional demands.

Hence the purpose of this book. The first chapter includes a brief overview of microphone styles and their convergence with African American blues and jazz. Factors influencing the evolution of vocal approaches, such as the nature of instrumental backup, recording studio technology, and live sound reinforcement, as well as speech and language considerations, are examined. Performing "on the gig" is also featured, including rehearsal techniques and suggestions from versatile professionals who've crossed over effectively. Strategies for learning songs quickly and accurately as well as achieving vocal longevity and endurance are also discussed. Chapter 2 furnishes practical real-world strategies for performing in intimate arenas (troubadour, duo, and rhythm section) as well as large-performance arenas (orchestra, big band, and rock band) while coping with the nature and scope of instrumental backup. Chapter 3 is devoted to crossing over into the classical vocal world, including techniques employed by instrumentalists who cross over. Chapters 4 and 5 address vocal pedagogy for microphone idioms, including commercial music and jazz, and explore contemporary issues related to vocal pedagogy in academe.

In the last three decades, advances in voice science and research have dramatically influenced approaches in vocal pedagogy. Nevertheless, only now have vocal pedagogues begun to explore alternative vocalism in a systematic fashion, exploring belting and musical theatre, but rarely introducing singing on microphone. Much of the pedagogy is derived from experimental research rather than from successful practitioners in the field. Just as the most prominent pioneers in vocal pedagogy shared their proprioceptive experiences, the experiences shared by successful vocalists within the less traditional idioms who are also knowledgeable about vocal production and physiology can contribute significantly to that body of work, furnishing yet another resource for aspiring professional vocalists within a changing profession.

The more versatile a vocalist, the more opportunities for professional performance (work). Over the course of an extended career, many professional vocalists, including many prominent ones, have gone on to personally explore new, uncharted vocal territory, encountering a breadth of sensory and artistic experiences and growing in the process. From an aesthetic point of view, if one regards style not merely as idiomatically differing inflections or quality changes but rather as representing a point of view or perspective that is reflected in the timbres, dynamics, and projection of text, then singing *authentically* in differing styles can be richly rewarding.

Acknowledgments

I learned a great deal about singers while on tour with Tops in Blue, as I was exposed to the Temptations' version of "Old Man River," gospel runs, soul rhythms, and blues fervor. I began to appreciate firsthand a distinct approach to music and singing that was oriented toward an aural–oral tradition, with emphasis on the experiential and expressive. To Tom Edwards, director of Air Force Entertainment, and to the many TIB "priors" (as well as the troupe that is out there now, performing for troops even as I write this), sincere thanks for your inspiring dedication.

I also learned (again empirically, through on-the-job training) from my fellow academic accounting instructors and supervisors at Sheppard AFB, whose guidance and encouragement were instrumental in pointing me further down the road toward the teaching profession. To all of them I owe a debt of gratitude.

I am indebted to all the wonderful musicians I encountered in the Dallas–Ft. Worth, Nashville, and greater Miami areas for what they taught me through association and by example, as well as the pedagogues I observed at the educational institutions I attended and where I served on the faculty. I would especially like to thank my colleagues at the University of Miami, who inspire me daily with their musicianship and commitment, and to express deep appreciation to Dean William Hipp for his support and leadership. Special thanks to the guys in the jazz faculty with whom I have the good fortune to serve, namely Whit Sidener, the able chairperson, Don Coffman, Ron Miller, Randall Dollahon, Doug Bickel, Dante Luciani, Gary Lindsay, Steve Rucker, and Gary Keller.

To Professor Larry Lapin, thank you for your consistent support and encouragement. One could not find a finer colleague and mentor. Warm thanks are also extended to all the students, present and past (especially those alumnae who kindly keep in touch), who continue to teach and inspire me.

I continue to learn immeasurably from my association (can it be twenty years?!) with my esteemed colleagues at the Professional Voice Institute, otolaryngologist Dr. Bruce Weissman, and speech pathologist and copresenter Vivian Topp. They are consummate professionals, and it has been fun and enlightening as they continue to share their significant insight into the workings of the human vocal mechanism. Thanks as well to Julie and Mary for their patient assistance.

I would like to express how grateful I am to those who contributed in wisdom and words by consenting to be quoted, including Jon Secada, Larry Lapin, Gary Keller, Glenn Basham, Wendy Pederson, Chris O'Farrill, Alex Pope Norris, Roseanna Vitro, Julie Jensen, Sheila Marchant Barish, and Bruce Miller.

And finally, to Mr. Michael D. Howe, I owe a special debt of gratitude for his forbearance and sustenance during the home stretch. Thank you, my very dearest neighbor.

∾

CHAPTER ONE

Crossing Over from Acoustic Idioms to Microphone Idioms

Power to Make Music

Evolution of Vocal Styles on Microphone

A new and very sensitive instrument which catches the buzzing and whispering usually heard in the background. Someone even has said that the new instrument will record the swish of a powder puff as it passes over the nose of some fair lady.

—"New Radio Rules," *Billboard*, April 1, 1922

Why is understanding the evolution of microphone idioms in conjunction with blues-derivative singing styles important? An examination of singing styles associated with blues recordings and the microphone provides insight into cultural and musical influences that converged and evolved over time. Just as classical vocal traditions reflect Western European musical traditions and are constantly evolving, microphone idioms also reflect a history and the confluence of cultural and technological developments. Vocal and stylistic approaches reflect those developments.

Microphone styles tend to be performer centered as opposed to composer centered and are oriented toward the aural and oral rather than the literal (Sidran 1971; Stearns 1958). They have been and continue

1

to be heavily influenced and enriched by the African American elements derivative of blues, including gospel, ragtime, R & B, soul, hip-hop, and rap. Technological advances continually transformed the idiom as the advent of the microphone initially liberated the singer from the exigencies of projection and contributed to the emergence of crooning as a vocal approach. Songs were keyed to accommodate a comfortable vocal range, allowing for a more intimate, conversational delivery that focused on the text. Recording technology and the radio disseminated recordings to a wider audience. Electrification of accompanying instruments, particularly the guitar, produced the electrified blues and derivative idioms (R & B, rock, and soul) and exacted increased projection and percussive delivery from the singer. Digital technology and the globalization of musical influences through the media, including the Internet, continue to influence and transform the sounds and styles of recordings and the microphone singer worldwide.

Microphone Styles: A Short History

> The impact of the microphone upon vocal technique and upon the articulation of song and text would have been immense in any case. That the coming of radio just happened to coincide with a growing awareness and acceptance of a new Afro-American musical idiom compounded and intensified the repercussions. . . . The microphone liberated him [the popular singer] from the burden of making himself heard over considerable distances in public places. Jazz liberated him from the precise pitches and more or less arithmetically calculated rhythms of European music, permitting him to order the words within a phrase in a manner closer to the natural melody and the natural rhythm of speech.
>
> —Henry Pleasants, *The Great American Popular Singers*

The following summary is not intended to serve as a comprehensive history of commercial idioms and artists. Rather, it is a chronological overview of the evolution of vocal technique and stylistic approaches brought about by cultural developments and interactions, the influence of dance rhythms, alterations of instrumental accompaniment, and technological advances. The vocalists highlighted serve as prominent representative models who were widely emulated. Singers considered by some to be seminal have inevitably been overlooked. However, works that detail the history of commercial/jazz idioms and their vocal exponents are listed in the references.

1. At the turn of the century, black and white performers exchanged musical elements in a process of imitation. At this time, songs were shouted to facilitate projection and were projected in the speaking range. Meanwhile, in New Orleans, an exchange of musical ideas between singers and instrumentalists and improvisation on African "sorrow songs" and "work songs" foreshadowed the blues and classic blues singers.

2. From 1920 to 1940, a period known as the Jazz Age, the blues got exposure through "race records" as the classic blues singers, including Bessie Smith, Ma Rainey, Alberta Hunter, and Mamie Smith, gained influence. Concomitantly, the invention of the microphone meant that vocal projection was no longer a major focus of concern, and crooning supplanted the shouted vocal delivery. A more conversational vocal sound was cultivated, which coincided with the recorded sounds of performers in movie musicals as well.

3. From the 1930s to the early 1950s the Big Band Era came into full swing, literally. During this time singers achieved celebrity status with big bands, and swing was the style that predominantly accompanied dance steps as well. Manifestations of jazz, including scat singing and instrumental imitation, were also evident. Many of the great jazz singers (only first name required) sang with big bands, including Bing, Frank, Ella, Sarah, and Joe, to mention a few.

4. By the 1950s, radio and television produced matinee idols, and vocalism reverted back to a mellow, lyrical, commercial sound. Teen idols (Bobby Vee, Annette Funicello, Paul Peterson, Frankie Avalon) were manufactured by record labels, resulting in a softening of the R & B influence with the popularization of "tepid crooners" (Pleasants 1974).

5. Concurrently, the connection of instrumental accompaniment and electricity (resulting in the electric guitar, bass, and piano) fused with the blues to produce rhythm and blues (now com-

monly referred to as R & B), which required a louder, aggressive, projected vocal output to compete with electricity. Major vocal influences emerged at this time, including Chuck Berry, Muddy Waters, and B. B. King.

6. Rock 'n' roll, as represented by Bill Haley and the Comets and Buddy Holly, and amalgamated with country influences through Jerry Lee Lewis and Roy Orbison, represented the white counterpart to R & B and coincided with the emergence of the teenager, a targeted demographic group. Elvis Presley represented the convergence of R & B, white and black gospel, country and western, and the blues. As a result, R & B influences were absorbed and manifested themselves in singing styles, including the use of falsetto by males, particularly in the vocal groups that began to emerge. White female vocal sounds, however, generally tended to remain more understated.

7. The 1960s and early 1970s saw a rejuvenation of R & B influences through the British invasion and the discovery of groups such as the Beatles, the most notable of these. Driving, powerful vocals returned, and female British vocalists like Lulu, Petula Clark, and Cilla Black, as well as Americans Linda Ronstadt, Leslie Gore, and Dusty Springfield, transformed female vocalism somewhat, introducing more emphatic and aggressive delivery. The Chiffons, the Shirelles, the Ronettes, and Patti LaBelle and the Bluebells were among the African American female vocal groups that became popular around this time, displaying aggressive vocal styling.

8. The 1960s and '70s also witnessed the emergence of soul, which seemed to represent a secularization of gospel. Soul was derivative of R & B but incorporated more evidence of gospel origins. As a result, artists at this time, including James Brown, Aretha Franklin, Stevie Wonder, and Ray Charles (who actually presaged it, serving as a bridge between R & B and soul) incorporated gospel inflections such as vocal slurs, growls, and falsetto in combination with accentuated attack into phrases.

9. Singer–songwriters, including Carol King, Simon and Garfunkel, James Taylor, Elton John, Billy Joel, and Joni Mitchell, performed original material with light voices that placed an

emphasis on communication of text and influenced the vocal landscape with understated, conversational vocals and soft rock.

10. Through his label, Motown, Berry Gordy assembled songwriters, artists, and vocal groups that remain a profound musical influence to this day. His slate included Smokey Robinson and the Miracles, Marvin Gaye, the Temptations, Stevie Wonder, The Jackson Five, and the Commodores as well as top female vocal groups such as the Supremes, the Marvelettes, and Martha and the Vandellas. Gladys Knight of Gladys Knight and the Pips, while not a Motown artist, was also a strong vocal influence at that time.

11. By the late '70s and early '80s, synthesis and other instrumental and technological advances were reflected in studio tracks as well as live performances, and disco and other dance styles appeared. Musical and lyrical content became subordinate to a driving dance rhythm. The major exponents, especially the Bee Gees, incorporated falsetto for intensity and projection, while female vocalists like Donna Summer, Gloria Gaynor, and Irene Cara displayed powerful chest voice and belted vocal production. Country artists also reached popularity, as slick studio production resulted in more mainstream acceptance.

12. The 1980s saw a continuation of the fusing of idioms. Gospel continued to exert a profound influence on all idioms, and contemporary Christian artists began to achieve popularity. Aggressive vocals and high-intensity levels were maintained, even on the ballads. Male solo singers, including James Ingram, Peabo Bryson, and Luther Vandross, employed extreme full voice at high ranges, liberal use of falsetto, growls, gospel runs, and other embellishments and effects to achieve intensity. Female vocalists, including Whitney Houston, Gloria Estefan, and Mariah Carey, tapped into the entire vocal range at high-intensity levels. Sequencers and other technology continued to represent a fertile source of new instrumental timbres, achieving complicated rhythmic tracks that resulted in complicated dance and Afro-Cuban rhythms, setting the stage for the Miami Sound Machine, DeBarge, and other dance-friendly artists. Punk rock, acid rock, progressive rock, and a profusion of other subsets in

rock appeared. Meanwhile, adult contemporary formats brought the vocals of Al Jarreau, Michael Franks, George Benson, and a host of others to the ears of heretofore light jazz aficionados.

13. The advent of the music video revolutionized the music industry, with the emphasis on the visuals and choreography at the expense of vocal performance. Sophisticated recording technology such as pitch bending and special effects engineered the vocal sound of performers such as Madonna and Janet Jackson, conditioning listeners' ears to processed vocals that complemented computerized instrumental tracks.

14. The marriage of oratory with rhythm as represented by rap illustrates the importance of language. Language and dialect are manipulated to produce a vocal idiom that represents an urban perspective and culture. The stylistic use of vocal attack, the repetition of onset, and phrasing that accommodates a rhythmic groove figure prominently. Audible breaths are accentuated as part of the vibe and are inherent in vocal articulation in rap, which continues to transform vocalism.

15. The turn of the twentieth century witnessed the infusion of international music influences as the Internet broke barriers and made the world smaller and our ears bigger. Vocal sounds are integrating varying cultural manifestations, including heretofore nonmainstream vocal qualities and inflections, international languages, exotic instrumentation, and fusion of classical with commercial influences, to mention but a few. Eclectic vocal influences will continue to result in assorted and disparate vocal qualities and expression that will compel adjustments in vocal pedagogy to address the advent of new sounds and styles.

African American Influences: Blues and Jazz

The esoteric world of musical arts contains considerable racial barriers. It also provides opportunities to address some of America's persistent and inescapable abiding social concerns. . . . The mystery of our shared racial legacy is a conundrum that is not easily unraveled, yet remains such an opportunity.

—Lourin Plant, "Singing African-American Spirituals:
A Reflection on Racial Barriers in Classical Vocal Music"

Henry Pleasant's book *The Great American Popular Singers* contains, in my opinion, one of the more incisive, authoritative, and objective analyses of African American musical influences (particularly blues and jazz) on American popular singing extant. (A detailed discussion of the sociological and cultural implications of what Johannes Riedel [1972] labeled "the appropriation/revitalization process" goes beyond the scope of this book, but sources are listed in the references for further exploration.) The orientation was toward the aural–oral aspect of music as opposed to the literal, and toward spontaneity and the "inherently communal nature of oral improvisation" (Sidran 1971). The process of imitation and exchange unconfined by a written script liberated vocalists and instrumentalists to achieve a high degree of inventiveness and the personalization of vocal and instrumental expression. These elements, as well as the inclination to scoop, slur, or flip into a note rather than attacking a note directly, are musical values that contrast sharply with the delicate onset of voice and precise intonation exacted in Western music. The result is a variety of short utterances with sharp or "percussive accentuations" (Steinhous-Jordan 2005), stylistic inflections, and embellishments that constantly evolve and that can contrast sharply with the vocalism taught at colleges and universities.

Table 1.1 is a comparison of traditional vocal and interpretive ideals with the performance objectives and values of microphone idioms.

Factors Influencing Microphone Styles and Idioms

Instrumentation

Singers are often regarded as second-rate musicians or divas because their focus can tend to be on their vocal performance rather than on the bigger musical picture. However, for vocalists who are also musicians, the music does not begin when they open their mouth and end when they stop singing, regardless of musical style or genre. They tend to display awareness of and involvement in the instrumental introduction and the musical ambiance as the stage is set.

Just as projection and breadth of performance are different if a classical vocalist sings with a full orchestra or with a piano accompanist, the nature of instrumentation influences the timbres, dynamics, and

Table 1.1. Comparison of traditional vocal and microphone idioms

Western European Influences	African American Influences
Composer centered	Performer centered
Acoustic	Microphone
Literal conforming to the music as notated	Aural–oral emphasis
Bel canto beauty of tone; avoidance of shouting, nasality, and harsh open sounds and disjointed registers as well as undue vehemence (Pleasants 1974)	Expressiveness, permitting extra sonorities (growls, cries, slurs, percussive sounds, etc.)
Objective voice	Subjective voice
Western European influences dominate	African American influences (blues)
Voice as instrument	Voice as conduit for text
Formalized language	Vernacular speech

inflections of the vocalist in microphone idioms as well. If singers are accompanied by the sustained lines and delicate articulations of strings, the vocal onsets into words and phrases and how they are sustained (degree of vibrato, tapered phrases) tend to correspond. In contrast, when singing with brass sections, with the tongued articulations of horns, vocalists tend to respond with articulated inflections in words and phrases to project and maintain intensity. Electric guitars, synthesizers, and sequencers tend to require singers to project more to assert the vocal timbre over electricity, and the overall presentation tends to be more expansive to balance the increased instrumental output. There is a corresponding largeness of delivery and presentation, not unlike the adjustments imposed on an actor when transitioning from subtle on-camera acting to live-stage performance. Whether the accompaniment is setting a rhythmic groove that the vocalist complements and phrases around or the phrasing accommodates a preset written accompaniment, the rhythmic interaction in mutual response to the rhythmic pulse contributes to a musical and integrated performance.

Speech and Language

The performance and interpretation of vocal music raise problems of a particular kind: two elements—a musical text and a literary text—

> must be analysed and then synthesized. . . . In vocal music, the sonor-
> ity and the rhythm of the words are an integral part of the music itself.
>
> —Pierre Bernac, *The Interpretation of French Song*

Research in speech suggests that there are correlations between speech and human emotions. For example, an individual who is excited tends to speak at a rapid rate, with significant modulation of the voice and a medium to high pitch level. At the opposite extreme, in a sensual environment (lights low, à deux) the speech rate tends to be more lan-guid, with more subtle modulation and at a comparatively low pitch level. When one is being intense and trying to be persuasive, enuncia-tion tends to be clearer, with the speaker literally minding his/her p's and q's (or to be more accurate, s's and t's).

In idioms and song material that represent conversational speech (for example, an intimate torch song or patter tune), the delivery sug-gests the same characteristics. In the words of Jon Eisenson (1985),

> On the emotional side, a markedly slow rate of utterance is associated with
> solemnity, depressed moods, and sadness or sorrow. A marked increase of
> rate is associated with happier states, lightheartedness, and heightened feel-
> ings. The heightened feelings, however, need not always be pleasant. Anger
> is usually expressed through an increased rate of utterance. . . . Changes in
> rate of behavior are related to our physiological states and associated muscu-
> lar activity.

Classical vocalists generally sing in at least three languages in addition to their native tongue, and each one must reflect the prosody of that language in union with the musical line. In setting text to music, great composers have already synthesized the elements to some extent, and it is up to the vocalist to infuse the emotion implicit in the drama. For microphone vocalists, the interpretation and phrasing are more per-sonal and spontaneous, and music, if written, serves as a point of depar-ture for individualized interpretation. Whether classical or on microphone, if the vocalist does not honor the natural rhythm, intona-tion, and stress of the language, the result is a stilted, mechanical-sounding delivery.

Notated music specifies the frequency (pitch), rate (tempo), duration (rhythm), dynamics, pauses (rests), and some facets of phrasing. Great melodies tend to underscore salient words in context, often making use of an agogic accent (notes of longer duration) and/or tonic accent (abrupt high notes or unexpected intervallic leaps). The degree of weight or stress on a note is not necessarily notated, however, and phrasing with equal weight and stress on all syllables, without honoring the natural prosody of the language, makes the lyric interpretation sound stilted and mechanical. In microphone idioms, when the singer is phrasing and interpreting the words spontaneously, an understanding of speech in emotional situations is pivotal to communication and expression.

On the microphone, intimate confidential vocal sounds and timbres travel to the ear of the listener, and subtle treatment of phrasing and enunciation can be directed to the listener. Language is pronounced in the vernacular, representing everyday speech, so the pure vowel sounds and vowel modification used in traditional vocal production would distort singing at speech level. The influence of highly individualized speech pattern characteristics such as regional accents and dialects also flavors microphone styles. Twangs, drawls, and other speech habits affect vocal tract configuration, particularly the articulators. Jaw position and movement, tongue position (whether flat, retracted, swallowed, and so on), and mouth position contribute to the idiomatic sounds of commercial styles. Being able to achieve folksy, uncontrived vocal utterances that are closely aligned to speech patterns while maintaining vocal technique that contributes to vocal clarity and endurance is the challenge for microphone singers.

Recording Studio Technology
Recording studio technology affords even further isolation of the voice from the instrumental tract. Sensitive microphones reinforce low-frequency energy that would be inaudible and transmits unvoiced acoustical noise that contributes to a richer vocal timbre. Mixing technology often includes a specialized engineer to process the vocal tract exclusively, adding high-frequency energy to reinforce sibilants and other signals. Studio wizardry enhances the sound of a vocalist who is singing at a very soft dynamic (not to mention pitch bending and other corrections if necessary) so that the sound nonetheless achieves presence and fullness. Since the vocal channel is boosted, the ability to project the

voice over dense background instrumental tracks is deemphasized. Much like an extreme close-up on camera, the voice is isolated as a timbre. Acoustical noise, heard as breathiness or huskiness, conveys itself to the listener with a quality of immediacy that commands attention. Listeners have been conditioned to hear enhanced sounds in movies, recordings, or live performances in terms of volume and extensity, with increased presence. (For an informative discussion of the impact of amplification on vocalization and listener perception, consult Richard Barrett 2005, 273–277.)

Musical Parameters

The history of microphone styles can be categorized as dance centered, text centered, techno centered, and performer centered. *Dance-centered tunes* are dominated by music for dancing, such as swing, disco, Latin rhythms, and specialty dances (twist, Macarena, and electric slide, to mention a few) in which the vocalist's role is secondary. At the opposite end of the spectrum, *text-centered tunes* in which the melody seems to be woven around the words, not infrequently presented by singer–songwriters on piano or guitar, place the focus on communication of poetic language, often original and didactic material that is rich with meaning. *Techno*, digital sampling, and other expanding computerized technology places the vocal lines amidst highly synthesized effects and electronic rhythms, lending a detached, programmed, automated effect. Hybrid styles, which seem to combine dance with performer-centered presentation in which the vocals are subordinate (either over-dubbed over prerecorded tracks or lip-synced), predominate particularly in the video era and in complex stage performances. Nevertheless, due in part to the individual vocalists who serve as idols (American idols, or otherwise), *performer-centered* music in which the singer is front and center, singing in real time and expressing shared human experience, will continue to thrive.

Crossing Over to the Mike: "On the Gig"

Through repetition, constancy, vocal health, and your performance effectiveness is how I have found to apply my training in whichever genre of singing I am dealing with at that moment.

—Jon Secada, personal communication, November 29, 2005

Vocal Performance on Microphone

If I'm doing a gig on microphone, the situation is as follows:

- The instrumental accompaniment sets a rhythmic groove (e.g., a medium swing or a languid 12/8 feel), producing it extemporaneously, rather than from a written detailed score. Regardless of the size of the band behind me, the microphone enables me to project even at relatively low dynamic levels for intimate passages.

- Since I don't have to tap into my soprano head voice and the resonant frequencies (the old 2800, the singer's formant) to project, I can keep the song within the speaking range as a point of departure. I don't need the sustained phonation of legato but can use a delivery that corresponds to the rhythm, intonation, and stress of speech, and I can include more vocal inflections.

- I sing in keys that correlate with my optimal speaking range and begin comfortably low in my range for low-intensity passages (often at the beginning of the tune), and my vocal intensity increases naturally as the melody ascends to the climactic passages of a song, corresponding with the intense notes in the voice range. (Note: Although the concept of optimal pitch has largely been discredited in speech pathology circles, the notion of an optimal pitch *range* has not been discarded.)

- Judicious key selection not only allows me to show off the meat of the voice but also to pace myself within a song and a gig. If the key is too high and requires vocal effort even at the start of the tune, with the attendant breath pressure, increased exertion is exacted by the time I reach the climactic notes, creating more opportunities for cracking, singing too heavily, and losing control. Performing in comfortable keys allows me to control dynamics vis-à-vis effort as opposed to muscular tension controlling me.

- My phrasing and rhythmic treatment, while integrating the outer rhythm and time feel, indicate the pulse (subdivision) as well so that I am at one with the rhythm section, particularly the drummer, regardless of the size of the group accompaniment.

- Having internalized the groove, I am then free to phrase spontaneously, blending the melody and lyrics in a manner that highlights each but sacrifices neither. Since I don't have to adhere to notated rhythms, I can be spontaneous, since I am expressing the lyric theoretically in the context of a scenario. Since many microphone idioms are derivative of rhythm and blues, soul, and gospel, words and phrases are initiated with inflections such as slurs, scoops, yodels and percussive consonants, runs, and other vocal embellishments. In aggressive styles the delivery is the antithesis of legato, with each word and often each syllable being accentuated.

- Melismatic embellishments, slurs, and other inflections entail some vocal flexibility and agility, so my attacks or onsets must be coordinated with the breath. In contrast to the extended classical legato phrase and the steady breath stream, in singing swing, rock, and other aggressively rhythmic styles, my breath pulsation must be coordinated with the enunciation of words and used for embellishments and ornamentation. Phrases and musical figures tend to be more condensed and accentuated with tenuto-like accents on words, rhythmic figures, and releases. All my utterances are mediated by the breath, but the breath stream is articulated like roulades and embellishments in coloratura passages.

- For ballads or styles characterized by moderate dynamics, the vocal folds are relaxed and flaccid in the comfortably resonant speaking range, so I am at liberty to experiment with various tone colors and vocal timbres. I can round the mouth and lips for a dark sound or achieve a brighter quality with a smiling sound. Vocal coloration and subtle adjustments in projection and enunciation produce nuances in vocal timbre and dynamics.

- The mike is also sensitive to puffs of air generated by consonants. In aggressive passages, I'll avoid excessive popping by adjusting the microphone. However, in warm, sensual passages, I might prolong voiced consonants like *l* and *v* on the word *love* or fricatives like *f* in *feel*, or click the final *t* or *k* of a word or phrase deliberately, but softly—a choice that might not be available to me when I sing acoustically.

- Dynamics on microphone can also be illusionary. I can use vocal production that projects sharply on microphone but that is rather anemic acoustically. Monitoring my vocal output through the monitors or speakers enables me to respond to the sound as it is picked up by the microphone and conveyed through the speakers and is vital to maintaining vocal control as well as vocal endurance, particularly before a large and loud instrumental accompaniment.

- The enunciation of vernacular speech (the predominant language in microphone idioms), or attempts to mimic everyday sounds, can result in poor vocal production, so coordination with the breath is my priority. I can discard pure classical vowel sounds when singing on mike (unless I'm really competing with loud electrified instrumentation), since it will distort the sound. The tongue does not have to lodge behind the lower front teeth to maximize projection but produces a wide spectrum of vocal qualities and actively produces final consonants at releases. Regardless of the vocal style (country, rap, alternative, etc.) my throat is open, my jaw is flexible and relaxed, and I utilize oral and mask resonance to project the sound, rather than muscular action. I should feel in control of all the qualities and dynamics in the style.

- As opposed to the delicate releases and tapering of phrases of traditional styles, jazz, rock, and other rhythmically aggressive styles dictate strong releases at the ends of phrases, which are integral to rhythmic integrity. Attention is given to variety in length as well as the way that the phrase is released (with the breath, not the throat!).

- A periodic vibrato present throughout the tone used by my classical counterparts is not often applicable in R & B styles and many microphone idioms. I'll use my vibrato predominately at the ends of phrases to add warmth and to complete a phrase gracefully. The vibrato is most effective and least obtrusive when it is in proportion to the vocal range and dynamic level of the tune. For example, on middle C, the rate and frequency will be discrete and more centered on the pitch than in singing C^5, the octave above. In that range, the ear will tolerate more pitch and amplitude variation.

- Ultimately, all the technical elements must be assembled and coordinated so that my delivery sounds spontaneous, heartfelt, and believable.

Crossing Over into Microphone Idioms
The challenges for classically trained vocalists who have never ventured into country, pop, R & B, or other popular music styles include

- Adjusting to microphone projection as opposed to projecting acoustically.
- Adjusting to singing in the speaking voice range and vernacular speech production.
- Phrasing and lyric interpretation that spontaneously deviate from the music as notated.
- Interacting (without intimidation) with the instrumentalists and musical accompaniment.
- Singing on the microphone—and not sounding too "legit."

The trademarks of a novice vocalist trying to cross over into singing in microphone idioms include the following:

Microphone technique. Difficulty monitoring the vocal sound as it emerges from the speakers, and making no adjustments in terms of range, dynamic control, vocal timbres, and vocal inflections.

Voice mode. Singing in the range and with vocal quality that, while guaranteed to project acoustically, distorts the sound on microphone and overwhelms the listener.

Language. Employing formalized English with pure vowels and artificial consonants rather than vernacular speech and inflection.

Phrasing and lyric interpretation. Interpreting the music and text literally from the printed music with vocal duration and stress accommodating note values rather than prosody of language. In short, phrasing sounds stiff. Attempting to imitate the original recording artist in the original or published key, in effect trying to sing with another person's vocal mechanism.

Vocal quality and style. Singing legato with emphasis on projecting a large vocal sound, employing vibrato throughout the tone. If female, using head voice resonance predominantly, and avoiding any midvoice or chest voice integration for nuance and color.

Interaction with instrumental accompaniment. Difficulty being aware of or keying into the rhythmic groove and pulse provided by the rhythm section as part of the entire performance picture.

Rehearsal Accompanist: Pianist versus Keyboard Player

> I only believed in one thing. Whatever you do has to be convincing at the time. Any musical performance has to be—not predictable, but inevitable. If it's predictable, it becomes cheap. If it's inevitable, then it's convincing.
>
> —"Janos Starker: A Cellist's Memoir" by Susan Stamberg

Perhaps an effective device to illustrate the adjustments inherent in making the transition from acoustic idioms to microphone idioms is to compare the experiences of two professional vocalists at an initial meeting with a keyboard accompanist. I assume that they are female vocalists to highlight the proprioceptive adjustments.

Acoustic Performances
In the acoustic situation, the vocalist presents classical works, usually opera, oratorio, or art songs with published piano accompaniment or score reductions. The repertoire reflects whether she is a lyric soprano, mezzo-soprano, or other classification as well as the size of the voice (lyric, dramatic) and vocal flexibility and agility. Since vocal production is designed to project acoustically and dynamically over orchestral, chamber, or piano accompaniment in performance venues of variable size, female vocalists employ head resonance and a vocal tone characterized by clarity, ring, and vibrato throughout the tone. The rehearsal space itself can range from a small studio to a recital or concert hall that enables the vocalist to calibrate vocal projection, shading, and balance. The experienced professional accompanist is more than likely familiar with the material, which can encompass any of at least four languages, and makes adaptations to the singer's interpretive elements, including breath marks related to phrasing and preferences in tempo. Ultimately, both musicians are on the same page, literally and figuratively, in keeping with a strong tradition of performance practice in classical vocal idioms. In the case of traditional musical theatre, positioning and a wider variety of interpretations may come into play, but the character roles are recognized and familiar, with the accompaniment written out.

Microphone Idioms

For the singer performing in a microphone idiom, the scenario is far less predictable for both vocalist and keyboardist. The vocalist can present a repertoire taken from various idioms, running the gamut from jazz, pop, R & B, country, rap, and retro (to name a few) to the music of the newest emerging global artists. As a consequence, the accompanist is challenged to be familiar with selections from a wider body of literature. Even if jazz is the idiom in question, standard repertoire can include up-tempo or moderate swing, traditional ballads, Brazilian, bebop, adult contemporary, and so on. In addition, since microphone idioms tend to be in the aural–oral tradition, songs are commonly written and recorded directly to tape rather than notated. Consequently, the rhythm section often makes use of a chord chart or a simple blueprint numbers chart or develops a spontaneous instrumental track by ear (this method still exists, particularly in Nashville). Later, the music is transcribed for the benefit of music publishers.

If printed, the music is published in keys that accommodate cheaper printing costs (simple, with fewer ledger lines, etc.) if it is printed at all. Consequently, reliable keyboard accompaniment is largely dependent on the ear of the keyboardist to transcribe in combination with the ability to read chord changes and by extension lead sheets or arrangements.

Since she has the use of a microphone, the vocalist will have selected a key that permits her to project a conversational tone, one that is pitched closer to her speaking range so that she can relax on the microphone for the lower notes and control the intensity in ascending passages of the melody. Logistically, a sound system with microphone should be available, unless it was understood that the duo would be re-creating a cabaret or jazz duo scenario with keys and vocal style that correspond to performance on mike.

Unlike his or her classical counterpart, the keyboard accompanist is the timekeeper and maintains a reliably steady tempo and rhythmic feel. This enables the vocalist to phrase freely, deferring to the rhythm of speech and maintaining the pulse inwardly, allowing the text to dictate how the melody is conveyed. In jazz and most popular idioms, projection of an aesthetically beautiful tone quality is subordinate to rhythmic feel and expressive lyric interpretation. Ultimately, the vocalist and keyboardist are collaborating to produce a spontaneous, creative rendition.

Thus, in the traditional, classical aesthetic, the map is laid out in detail, and it is up to the vocalist to render an interpretation that can be described as sounding, in the words of the great cellist Starker, "not predictable, but inevitable" (Stamberg 2004).

Conversely, notwithstanding the improvisatory and aural–oral orientation of the microphone style, the vocal rendition, while unstructured, can also become inevitable but not predictable.

Proprioception: Suggestions from Versatile Vocalists Who've Switched

Discussions and technical work with experienced classical and musical theatre performers and teachers who had not previously worked in microphone idioms have afforded me an opportunity to hear their responses and adjustments as they perceived them while exploring mike technique. Being pedagogues themselves, they were better able to perceive and articulate the kinesthetic feedback and adaptations necessary in response to vocal and stylistic demands.

The following are some of the observations regarding sensory feedback in crossing over as well as strategies to accommodate the demands of microphone idioms.

Find a favorite song. One of the quicker means to an interpretive end is to imitate vocal renditions by vocalists who seem to approximate your vocal approach or a style and sound for which you have some affinity. A sound is worth a thousand words, and by imitating a favorite singer and his or her vocal and stylistic inflections, you get the opportunity to wear the rhythmic feel, musical vibe, and style, and your body should respond reflexively to achieve the target sound and delivery.

Put it in the speaking range. Singing that uses the speaking voice range engenders the most radical adjustments for a female classical singer. Employing the term *speaking voice* rather chest voice is deliberate. Speech patterns that are resonant and supported incorporate optimal pitch levels and balanced muscular action at a moderate dynamic level. That is why it might be helpful to casually sing the song a cappella at the speech level with a lot of modulation at a medium dynamic level. You can croon a ballad or, if you're comfortable (and can let go more easily), surrender to the natural prosody of the language. You might use a patter tune or light rock tune that taps in somewhat to your alter ego. While it may be helpful to listen to another artist's rendition at the outset, you should resist singing along with the artist, since the key may not correlate with your natural comfort range. Singing the tunes a cappella in a vocal range that is comfortable for your individual instrument helps you to feel more spontaneous physically, vocally, and stylistically.

Don't worry about projection. Don't be preoccupied with vocal projection at this point. When you sing reflexively at speech level, the dynamics tend to take care of themselves on the mike, as a reflection of attitude, whether it be sensual and intimate, or aggressive and declamatory.

Don't get too heavy. Let the mike empower you. Be aware of the tendency initially to get too heavy with the sound and the vocal mechanism. It might be useful to introduce the microphone into the proceedings at this point in time. This can be relaxing for some, but can be disorienting for others, since it introduces adaptations, distractions, and monitoring responses into the mix that could prove overwhelming at this juncture.

The lyrics are the point. If you're having difficulty forgoing legato, concentrate on the rhythm of the language, which takes precedence. You might sense the text as sounding choppy as you're imitating trumpets rather than violins, but your inflections of words and phrases will help you sound more natural. According to Bruce Miller, acting coach, "The greatest singers in every genre, from any point in the history of singing, all share the ability to use their lyrics as effectively as they use the music those lyrics fly with" (1999).

You can maintain your individual sound, accents and all. Being able to keep your regional accent and other manifestations of your individual sound can contribute to a unique quality, assuming that your speech pattern is not unduly unhealthy. Remnants of your speech pattern can (and perhaps should) be maintained. For example, tight-tongued country, a folksy twang, or the gospel slurred breath need not interfere if the vocal tract is open and coordination with the breath and resonance are optimal.

Eliminate poor speaking habits and associated tension. If your habitual speech displays abusive habits (glottal attack, retracted tongue, tight jaw, etc.), they will inevitably manifest themselves in vocal fatigue and disorders. They need to be attenuated, preferably in speech, so that you can integrate them naturally when you're singing without them detracting from your performance. According to Vivian Topp, speech pathologist, "Singers tend to understand about voice conservation and voice use. However, people who entertain with their voice also are entertainers when they talk. They don't realize that they are overusing their voices. Singers tend to be affective speakers" (Personal communication, June 2005). A balance between preserving an individual's unique sound and maintaining vocal endurance is the challenge. Notwithstanding, singers who have been able to achieve a wide spectrum of sounds and styles and thrive within various musical idioms have enjoyed illustrious and enduring careers. It is good practice to consult a certified speech pathologist or other voice professional if abusive vocal behaviors have been identified or when you have concerns.

It's not only about your sound! One of the biggest challenges for a classical-trained vocalist initially is to subordinate vocal sonority to text. The most direct way to emphasize style over sound is to focus on the words as the conduit for the voice. Separating the elements and transcribing the words on a sheet of paper in the form of a poem (also the ideal opportunity to add it to your lyric book) places the lyrics front and center, literally and figuratively. It also facilitates memorization and can offset the tendency on the part of those who have some level of photographic retention to be literal, to phrase and accent music exactly as notated. You might also start with a very intimate, introspective ballad, singing it rubato.

If you work to breathe, it won't work for you. Breath management should introduce itself automatically in terms of phrasing and intention. Inhalation should also be in proportion to the phrase and be part of the rhythm and prosody of the words and music. As described by Michele Weir, "The breath taken before the start of any given phrase should reflect the mood of that phrase. In other words, the flavor of a phrase begins with the character of the breath attached to it" (2005).

Get comfortable with the mike. The microphone can represent a hurdle, particularly as you try to respond to your voice as it comes out of the sound speakers. The reaction is to reflexively pull away from the mike and pull back on the volume. However, microphone idioms should be rehearsed on microphone so you can become acclimated to the vocal input vis-à-vis the output as conveyed through amplification. (For more detailed information, refer to the section on the microphone in Lebon 1999.)

Work with instrumentalists. Avail yourself of the opportunity to work with a pianist, rhythm section, or prerecorded studio tracks. Singing with accompaniment introduces a host of new proprioceptive adjustments. Current technology affords multiple ways to acquire musical tracks in congenial keys. However, a track can be predictable once you have heard it numerous times. This makes it easier to yield to a predictable, safe imitation (as this adjudicator can attest, having heard innumerable derivative renditions of a certain tune based on one single popular and overused instrumental track!). Getting together with live musicians can stimulate inventiveness and freshness while you interact and respond to living, breathing instrumentalists making music together.

Strategies to Learn Songs Quickly, Accurately, and Musically
1. Scope a tune: Have a pencil and mark your music!
2. Learn the melody: Use the Nashville number system, which
   - Enables you to accurately learn and retain a melody (or transcribe one) regardless of key and lack of scoring paper.
   - Allows you to place the melody (in numbers) in your lyric sheet.
3. Learn the lyrics: Type a lyric sheet immediately, which
   - Allows you to isolate the lyrics from the music, rather than subordinating them to the music.
   - Brings out the lyrics as poetry and as an expression of ideas.
   - Reinforces the prosody (rhythm, intonation, and stress) of the language, avoiding text delivery that sounds stilted and mechanical.
   - Allows you to free the phrasing from the written text, particularly if you are visual.

4. Memorize: Avoid singing along with the recording to internalize the tune. Remember:
   • You tend to push vocally to sing over the original artist.
   • The recording may not be in or close to your ideal key!
   • You are being cued into phrases, resulting in false security in memorizing lyrics.
   • You are acquiring *someone else's* melody, which may be an adaptation.
   • You are not analyzing the melody and lyrics independently, which would enable you to acquire a personalized interpretation.

   Rather, you should be singing aloud in real time, reinforcing tactile memory by enunciating the words.

5. Acquire a personalized interpretation: Isolate the elements of a song by
   • Singing the melody on a vowel, like an instrument.
   • Speaking the lyrics as a monologue.
   • Weaning yourself away from various artists' interpretations of a particular tune as you assume your own perspective or scenario, though you can listen to various renditions and interpretations.

6. Apply yourself to being able to learn and internalize a song or jingle in the short term: Mark your music copiously with numbers or intervals for notes, rhythmic reminders, cutoffs at ends of phrases, and so on, so that
   • You do not repeat the same mistakes during rehearsals.
   • You have a tangible, visual reminder of tricky rhythms, melodic leaps, and releases.
   • You make use of your knowledge of sequences, repeated phrases, or motives, and so on to analyze the music.

7. "Buzz" the lyrics: Use clear enunciation and phrasing that communicate ideas with assurance (rather than being tentative) and contribute to a believable rendition of a tune.

8. Acquire your individual repertoire: Keep songs fresh for the long term. Your song repertoire indicates your dedication, preparation, musical identity, and artistry. Remember to

- Learn a song accurately and thoroughly the first time, and it will remain with you.
- Have a repertoire sheet with songs available, organized by style or idiom, plus keys (sometimes a choice of two, depending on the performance situation and your vocal condition).
- Refrain from showing a song as part of your repertoire unless you can perform it immediately, persuasively, and with style under all circumstances.

9. Sing in an ensemble: Making music together or ensemble (which literally means "together" in French) means that you depend on each other. Remember:
   - Have a pencil and mark your music!
   - Avoid merely pounding notes on the piano to learn parts. Use numbers to learn melody or solfège as a reminder of the function of your note in the chord to enhance tuning.
   - Mark releases, articulations, rhythms, and changes or adjustments immediately so that they become habituated.
   - Make sure everyone knows the music. If only a single individual member does not know the music, the ensemble does not know the music.
   - Become secure about all aspects of the music. Performers who are insecure with parts, lyrics, or mechanics will not communicate or perform with conviction and energy.

Achieving Vocal Longevity and Endurance

As a member of the Professional Voice Institute, an interdisciplinary team devoted to the treatment of vocal disorders, I have been fortunate to interact with distinguished vocalists from the worlds of Broadway, the recording studio, and live performance as well as with voice-over artists, DJs, and on-camera talent who have enjoyed extended careers. As working professionals in the true sense of the word, they take pride in their ability to nurture and maintain their instruments through abusive schedules and demanding vocal roles. Notwithstanding their conscientious vocal hygiene practices and solid vocal technique, the convergence of circumstances beyond their control can sometimes contribute to vocal fatigue and dysfunction.

Seasoned pros display a sense of wounded pride at having to

acknowledge that they have run into some difficulty. Adverse conditions in the performing environment compounded by stressful lifestyle changes seem to be factors when established singers with thriving performing careers encounter vocal difficulties. Some specific situations in the realm of the performance setting include

- The requirement to sing in set keys and ranges that accommodate the accompanist, prerecorded tracks, or the original artist, resulting in vocal fatigue and strain.
- Abusive rehearsal schedules performed full voice, with no marking or apportioning of vocal energy to preserve the voice so that it is not in optimal shape for performance. A survey of professional casting agents, Broadway producers, cruise ship directors, and other professionals employing singers suggested that "many did not understand their technique enough to sustain eight shows a week" (Alt 2004).
- Abusive itineraries and performance schedules that cross time zones and the associated physical stresses (dehydration, lack of sleep, jet lag) related to them.

When these elements interact with lifestyle changes and the attendant stressors associated with them, vocal disorders can manifest themselves. Prime examples include

- A cold, flu, or virus without the singer taking sufficient rest or recuperation time, which affects the immune system in the long term, and creates a predisposition for relapse. Often patient complaints are traced back to such an episode in which the singer performed with a cold or returned to performance prematurely, before recovering fully.
- Sudden and drastic weight changes, dieting or change in diet, or loss of weight brought on by stress. Being stoic and going on with reduced physical energy and compromised breath control can often result in excessive laryngeal involvement and vocal fatigue.
- Emotional stress brought about by life changes complicated by other issues (divorce, relocation, children, etc.). Shallow respira-

tory patterns and heightened muscular tension promote vocal inefficiency and voice problems.

- Maturation and physiological changes related to age figure prominently in alterations in vocal responses, as the vocal mechanism is constantly evolving and calcifying. The high notes and resiliency enjoyed courtesy of youth are not as cooperative as we age, necessitating proprioceptive as well as attitude adjustments. Allergies and poor lifestyle habits, which youth allowed us to get away with nearly unscathed, have a more pronounced effect on the voice as we age, and flexibility and agility (as well as confidence) are not as reliable. Vibrato is also more difficult to control.

The question of whether microphone (nonclassical) singers are more prone to vocal disorders is a controversial one. Resourceful and talented vocalists in microphone idioms can subconsciously make adjustments when their voice is fatigued, either by substituting for climactic passages, lowering keys, or increasing the sound amplification levels. Since the singer can style around difficult passages or substitute for extreme high notes (the initial signs of vocal problems), the vocal deterioration is gradual and undiscerned as the singer compensates by working harder, resulting in further erosion of the vocal mechanism and vocal disorders. Microphone singers can remain functional at the professional level for quite a while, and when they finally seek help, their complaints usually involve an obvious register break not present before, loss of breath control (due to air leakage from imperfectly adducted folds), and loss of endurance.

~

CHAPTER TWO

Microphone Singing in the Performance Arena

The Intimate Performance Arena

The "Troubadour": The Self-Accompanied Singer–Songwriter

Performing songs that can encompass a wide range of genres, from country to blues to folk to Celtic rock, and so on, while self-accompanied on guitar or piano, represents the continuation of a long tradition of troubadours or singer–songwriters. Artists run the gamut from Billy Joel and Joni Mitchell to Carol King and Tom Lehrer, to name but a few—self-accompanied musicians who constitute a "triple threat" (Alt 2004) by writing their own songs. Original tunes sung to one's own musical accompaniment obviates the necessity for notated music and allows one to assert a measure of control. Adding home studios to that mix and marketing through the Internet provide many more opportunities for exposure—more than just the neighborhood pub. Proficient vocally as well as on their axe, singer–songwriters often use the guitar, piano, or even bass (Kristin Korb, for example) as a source of inspiration for some songs, weaving melody and lyrics around an instrumental groove. In the words of Raul Midon (equally virtuosic on guitar and on vocals), "It's just a matter of coming up with a cool riff and putting words to that" in developing some tunes (Montagne and Kahn 2005). Troubadours are preoccupied with vocal production to the extent that it serves as a vehicle to transmit their song material—material that can be didactic, clever, reverent, or comical with a payoff ending, and sometimes all within the same tune. Ultimately, much of the listener's attention is directed to the lyric rather than the sound of the singer–songwriter.

Preparation: Acquiring Mastery over Vocal and
Instrumental Elements in Isolation
While *you* are intimately familiar with your own material, which will have undergone many revisions in developmental stages, your listener, on first hearing, is not. Therefore, clear communication of lyrics and independence from the demands of self-accompaniment are important. You can best accomplish this by isolating the instrumental accompaniment to achieve facility and by practicing the melody and lyrics a cappella to become comfortable with the ebb and flow of the language. Once both elements are combined, the whole becomes more than the sum of its parts, and the lyrics communicate more effectively to the listener. Otherwise, a strong instrumental accompaniment can overwhelm and obscure the lyrics.

Practice enough on the instrument (guitar or piano) so that you achieve tactile memory and fluidity without hesitation or hiccup in the accompaniment that would distract from the vocals. The same applies to internalizing the vocals. As critic and writer Ashley Kahn remarked in describing Midon, "His singing doesn't slow down as he works the strings" (Montagne and Kahn 2005).

Rehearsal: Communication of Text, Pacing, and Variety
In music that is lyric centered, singing in a key that optimizes natural resonance and freedom of articulation goes a long way toward ensuring intelligibility. Sometimes keyboard players or guitarists sacrifice a congenial key for the voice in favor of one that is comfortable for playing their axe. The result is fewer vocal choices in terms of timbre and dynamics, with reduced intelligibility.

While you may seek to communicate the lyric in a natural, uncontrived manner, maintaining clarity in enunciation should remain a priority. This underscores the importance of keeping the text fresh through the emphasis on different word choices and thinking about what you're saying while you're singing it. "Buzzing" important words by the manner in they are pronounced or singing the phrase with attitude while conforming to "speech rhythm" (Lapin 2004) can give the lyric a life of its own that, when unified with the music, provides more impact.

In interpreting other writers' material or doing covers (which can place you at a disadvantage since your listeners are conditioned to hearing the original interpretation), a creative take on a standard that is motivated by a fresh perspective or attitude can give the impression that the words are being discovered or reinterpreted at that precise moment, enabling the audience to temporarily forget the original and pay attention to you rather than dismissing your performance as unremarkable.

Performance: Putting It All Together
Verify that your posture, whether singing at the piano or with a guitar strap over your shoulder, is optimal. Pianists should sit at the piano with the mike positioned so that they avoid lifting the chin or caving in at the torso. Guitarists should avoid slouching and sit erect so that they can connect with the breath source. Microphone position and mike stand should enable the vocalist to sit up or stand straight and comfortably.

While, theoretically, self-accompanied singers need not contend with instrumentalists who wouldn't mind covering up the vocals, you should nonetheless be mindful of balance between your voice and your accompaniment. Sound speakers and monitors should be positioned so that you can monitor yourself. This ensures that you project with clarity and without undue exertion over ambient noise, which might be considerable in certain performing environments. The same applies to instrumentalists who sing in bands.

Changing tempo, textures, and timbres, for example, adding a cappella sections to provide space, commands attention and injects variety. Pauses, hits, spoken sections, snaps, and mouth percussion are all devices that change texture and provide interest. Dynamic variation is also important, as is pacing throughout the set, since you cannot rely on the addition or elimination of instruments to change the texture. Being unpredictable and providing a variety of moods, attitudes, and some humor while keeping your listeners hanging on your every word

are the trademarks of a special singer–songwriter and a successful troubadour.

Vocal Technique Applications for the Singer–Songwriter
Projection and dynamic range. You can be intimate since you don't
have to compete with other instrumentation. Use a variety of dynamics
to maintain interest. Balance instrumentation with vocals so that lyrics
project clearly to the listener.

Attack and breath management. Coordinate consonants for clarity.
Support vernacular speech efficiently at a medium dynamic.

Time feel and phrasing. Customize your phrasing since you're self-
accompanied and can accommodate your own pace, phrases, and so on.
Avoid straightjacketing yourself with the music as you wrote it. Be
flexible and lyric centered, adhering to the rhythm of the words but not
at the expense of accompaniment.

Vocal timbre and inflection. Use scoops, growls, yodels, and other
stylistic devices liberally, as suggested by the musical material. Use
effects on the instrument (plucking inside the piano or slapping the
guitar) to provide variety.

Lyric interpretation and style. Remember that you are very familiar
with the words and vibe of your tune, but your listeners are not. Clarity
and attention to what you are saying in the moment creates a quality
of immediacy that is seductive. In a performance venue with a lot of
ambient noise, you can draw the customers in and command attention.

Applied voice. Maintain your personalized, individual, unique
sound, but make sure that vocal idiosyncrasies and vocal effects do not
result in vocal erosion. Watch posture and sit upright. Pianists should
avoid raising the chin to meet the mike. Maintain an angle so that the
entire body is shifted toward the audience and the neck does not turn
alone. Guitarists should avoid slouching over the guitar from the weight
of the strap or for any other reason. Microphone positioning is important in helping you stay coordinated with the breath.

Rehearsal techniques. Isolate musical elements so that the vocal
does not become subservient to the instrument, or vice versa. Cultivate
proprioception for both. Use pauses, instrumental effects, and varied
timbres liberally and rehearse in real time, particularly original songs,
so that you can pace your material.

The Duo: A Musical Partnership

When a singer–songwriter feels straightjacketed vocally and instrumentally by the need to furnish musical accompaniment, venturing into duo territory could prove to be very satisfying artistically. One of the most musically rewarding experiences for a vocalist is performing in a duo with a pianist or guitarist who appreciates singers. When two musicians sense a certain artistic rapport and can establish a unified objective in mood and pacing, the result can be richly rewarding.

Preparation: Establishing a Unified Objective in Mood and Pacing

Both members of a duo must have thoroughly scoped the tune and become secure musically with the melody, lyrics, chord changes, and the generalized form of the tune (32 bars, through-composed, etc.). Ideally you should agree on the selection as a fertile source of creative ideas for exploration, with flexibility implied as the arrangement and interpretative elements develop. Ultimately, each rendition of the tune should develop in new directions and create its own distinctive mood.

Rehearsal: Interaction and Partnership

In a duo situation, "both instruments are very exposed, so you can experiment with new sounds and ideas, but you must be confident with the situation in order to do so" (Tini and Tini 1994). In such a transparent texture, you should become comfortable with the notion of pauses and musical space. You should use the lyrics as a guide to phrasing, and the pianist or guitarist should be aware of the text and respond to the interpretation. Singers cannot be insecure musically but need to "shed the tune" so that they can sing with conviction, sensitivity, and impeccable intonation. A pianist or guitarist will feel free to include complex chord progressions or "play with the time" if your vocal demeanor suggests that you are musically secure, are not easily thrown off key, and are flexible and receptive in terms of creativity and experimentation. Your phrasing and lyric interpretation should never be tentative or the instrumentalist will respond in kind. Within a cabaret setting, where the musical theatre influence may imply more literal piano accompaniment, the pianist will respond with subtle adjustments of touch and dynamics.

Performance: Spontaneity and Generosity While
Listening to Each Other

Within this setting, interaction is particularly crucial, since there is a
lot of opportunity for rubato (meaning, literally, stealing time, or
freely). Many ballads, even with a rhythm section or big band, open
with a verse or rubato section, so experience in singing freely yet in a
way that allows the instrumentalist to anticipate you in some contexts,
while giving you time to pause, is indispensable. Once each member of
the duo is reassured that the other is technically proficient, the resul-
tant interaction between vocalist and instrumentalist, as both relax and
they begin to trust each other, is exciting and musically satisfying for
both performer and listener.

The sense of musical trust having been established, both parties will
feel confident, bouncing ideas off each other (true indicators that they
are truly listening to each other) and generating freedom to explore a
spectrum of vocal colors and timbres. Rhythmic security can also lend
itself to experimentation with tempo and time feel, resulting in spontaneous, new arrangements every time. Rehearsals should merely constitute run-throughs or possible avenues for exploration that will evolve
and be transformed with each performance. The less that one member
dictates creative directions and the more equal the partnership, the
more collaborative and creative the result. Singing with solo piano, guitar, or bass can be one of the more exciting musical experiences for a
vocalist.

Vocal Technique Applications as a Duo

> Listen to each other, take advantage of the unique situation (be cre-
> ative!), and be inspired by great recordings.
>
> —April and Dennis Tini, "The Vocal/Piano Jazz Duo"

Projection and dynamic range. Be aware of the dynamic contrast
within a single song. In this intimate setting, a wide spectrum of
dynamics is possible with subtle nuances in vocal shading. The pianist
responds to the vocal line, but you should listen for surges and changes
in dynamics in the accompaniment. The guitar duo implies a comparatively narrower dynamic range, dictating subtlety and more space and

pauses. Acclimate yourself to feeling exposed in such a transparent texture.

Attack and breath management. Tap into breathy, intimate, nuanced vocal qualities, since projection is not an issue. Duos are more exposed, so audible inhalation can be distracting and, in view of the light accompaniment, unnecessary.

Time feel and phrasing. Be in character for some selections. Singing in a duo is very text oriented, so this is useful in generating phrasing ideas. Use lots of time travel, that is, staggered entrances and give and take. Concentrate on the pulse in rhythmic passages. Rubato passages need clarity of intention so that the accompanist can anticipate and respond.

Vocal timbre and inflections. Use inflections of speech, with the prosody of speech. Alternate between quick, clipped passages and sustained, gentle releases on sensitive ballads. Keep in mind that using a dissonant note on a sustained word for effect or selecting an extension on a final note demands an adjustment in harmony and chord voicings by the instrumentalist.

Lyric interpretation and style. Have a definite take and strong characterization on the text, and on each word, and microphrase (two or three words within the phrase). In a transparent texture, each word is loaded (with meaning), and pauses are also revealing. Each song is its own world and takes its own direction. *Listening* and playing off each other helps you sound spontaneous rather than contrived.

Applied voice. You can use vocal subtlety but also be theatrical, with sudden changes in dynamic levels. You need to have secure intonation and time feel to compete with the piano sonorities. Every new duo situation will (and should) generate new responses, whether with guitar or piano, and you must be flexible musically and vocally. Keep an ear on the kinds of attack used by the instrumentalist and complement them.

Rehearsal techniques. Bounce ideas off each other in rehearsals. Prepare each other for any radical changes in direction within the musical form ("I may start swinging here") so that there is some sense of shaping. Some instrumentalists are comfortable with genuine spontaneity, while others prefer a broad plan that is subject to alteration or tweaking in the moment of performance. Be mindful of the distinction between being spontaneous and being unpredictable. Easing into a slow swing from rubato is spontaneous; breaking into a fast swing abruptly without warning is unpredictable. Failing to listen or respond to the vibe and mood of your musical partner can undermine the collaborative effort.

The Acoustic Trio or Rhythm Section

If you are a singer–songwriter or part of a duo, the rhythmic feel is relatively free, with much rubato and no need to maintain a steady time feel. The addition of double bass and drums alters the performance scenario significantly, as the trio furnishes a steady beat the vocalist can play off of. Adding the electric guitar or any electrification converts the acoustic trio into a rhythm section, which for our purposes means keyboards (electric or acoustic), electric bass, electric guitar, and drums. The additional instrumentation represents more sound behind you, necessitating increased vocal projection.

Preparation: The Rhythm Sections Groove

Even when you sing with a big band, string orchestra, or rock band, the basic rhythm section (RS) forms the core of the ensemble and largely dictates the groove and energy. Each member of the RS contributes specifically, functioning within the interacting elements. The drummer is the timekeeper, setting up a good rhythmic feel and punctuating cadences, while the pianist plays harmonic chord progressions and melodic fills. The bass player lays down the harmonic foundation while serving as a bridge rhythmically and harmonically. If electric bass is used, the stylistic and dynamic palette is larger, while the acoustic bass is more intimate. The drummer also delineates form through fills and setups at cadences and ends of sections. The singer with "big ears" can key in on the different instrumental elements, integrating them and melting into the time, vibe, and dynamic levels. (For more information, refer to Michele Weir's discussion of the rhythm section in chapter 12 [2005]).

Rehearsal: Blueprints, Lead Sheets, or Arrangements

Increased instrumentation means that a clearer blueprint is needed for performance. Lead sheets or arrangements are a point of departure. The vocal musician should make a decision regarding the bookends (introduction and end) of a tune rather than deferring to the band. You can save time in rehearsals by running through the music with the pianist first to identify potential trouble spots and clean up the mechanics of intros and endings, the most important sections of the tunes, and the climax.

For many artists, the pianist functions as the musical director as well as the leader of the rhythm section and may have arranged the music as well. Good arrangements have a variety of textures and alterations in feel, which add form and interest. The sensitive singer complements changes in texture for a richer presentation. The addition of drums adds myriad rhythmic feels, grooves, timbre choices (high hat or ride cymbal), and techniques for indicating rhythmic subdivisions.

Being comfortable with the song form of the tune is essential, since you do not want to be a vocalist who is the proverbial joke, "knocking on the door but can't figure out when to come in." Having the lyrics in a format that corresponds to the song form can be very helpful in familiarizing yourself with it, along with writing the lead sheet yourself with rehearsal letters. Being armed with a mental outline of the arrangement enables you to be authoritative and confident before a rhythm section.

Performance: Together from Beginning to End
It's important for the vocalist to set up the time feel and vibe with the count-off clearly so that the introduction immediately reflects the mood of a song. You should take time to ensure that the tempo is the one that you want to work with by

- Singing and saying the words mentally. The rhythm and muscle memory of pronouncing the words is a reliable way to achieve a relatively consistent tempo.
- Being aware that in pressure situations, we can tend get a bit up-tempo. Avoid rushing.
- Counting off with flair and attitude, which sets up the vibe and transfers your energy and tempo clearly to the RS.

The singer's demeanor and internalization of the time feel should transfer itself to the rhythm section. According to Larry Lapin (2004), a member of the International Association for Jazz Education (IAJE)

Teacher Training Institute, "One of the weaknesses of inexperienced singers and players is that, too often under the heading of 'phrasing,' the soloist forgets that the pulse and time generation is as much his/her responsibility as that of the rhythm section or accompanist." Once the RS has established a nice time feel in a comfortable tempo, you can melt into the ambiance set and phrase freely, since it is the responsibility of the RS for keeping time, or to provide "firm although not rigid support" (Lapin 2004).

Special attention needs to be accorded the beginning of the tune, the intro, which is designed to

- Capture attention.
- Set the mood.
- Encourage the listener to maintain interest and empathy.

Once you've established the intro, the RS will feel free to be creative and engage in a musical dialogue, which adds richness to the presentation. The manner in which you render a rubato intro determines whether the listener hangs there with you or dismisses you and tunes out. The benefits are two-fold:

- A solid intro engenders respect on the part of the instrumentalists.
- Your performance will emanate assurance and conviction from the start.

In the case of an extended instrumental introduction (or a rubato intro played by the keyboard player), if you're insecure with your entrance, a perfunctory intro results and you are off to a tentative start. Familiarize yourself with the chord progressions, and get used to thinking in terms of 8-bar phrases.

The way you end a tune is the way you leave your audience. Do they feel that you've changed from the beginning of the tune to the end? Do they feel left in the air, with no conclusion? Have you encapsulated an experience or emotion with which they can identify? The inexperienced vocalist is exposed by the tendency to

- Rush the ending, and not hold the moment.
- Fail to pause before the final statement.

- Rush the final phrase so that the final note cannot be comfortably sustained.

An unprepared ending that seems to come to a screeching halt leaves the audience unsatisfied and undermines what may have been a powerful rendition of a song. You should prepare specific ideas about the song ending so you can bring it to a strong conclusion.

Being comfortable with the form of the tune is essential. Having the lyrics in a format that *corresponds to the song form* is very helpful in familiarizing yourself with it. A lead sheet or arrangement with rehearsal letters can help you be authoritative and confident before a rhythm section. If you're just sitting in, know the song form, key, tempo, and time feel for the count-off, and be prepared to broadcast your ending or listen for cues from the band for a

- Tag, with a distinctive cadence that leads you to a repetition of the final phrase
- Three-peat, which is the final phrase repeated three times
- Restatement of the final phrase rubato

It's always a good idea for the singer to be part of the ending chords, with a soft "ah" or "oo" that blends into the final sustained chord before release. Whether you sing the last word or a light vocalese, you want to have full control of your final note. You always want to end a tune gracefully.

When you're well versed on the mechanics of a song, the result is a more relaxed rendition that shows conviction. The band will feel free to play with feeling, to be creative, and to engage in a musical interchange, which adds richness to the presentation, so that when you join them, the feeling will be mutual.

Vocal Technique Applications with Acoustic Trio or Rhythm Section

> Music is best as conversation, not as group monologue; give space a chance. You can't hear the band as a whole if you're constantly playing; don't play on autopilot, react to soloists and watch the leader.

> —Roseanna Vitro, "Vocalists Are from Venus: Instrumentalists Are from Mars"

Projection and dynamic range. The addition of bass and drums entails more intensity, but also more rhythmic support. The RS at full throttle requires that you increase your projection and power. Arrangements should incorporate changes in texture and vocal pacing. For instance the drums can be introduced gradually, or the tune can open with just bass. This is particularly important for a full rhythm section, with both chordal instruments creating a heavy texture. Guitarists and pianists are especially aware of stepping on each other's territory, and the best ones strive to be sensitive, knowing when to lay out or play a supportive role. If you're doing a head arrangement, some discussion beforehand regarding a mixture of textural ideas in combination with dynamic changes is important to avoid monotony.

Attack and breath management. More sound behind you requires more output, and by extension, more breath support. Internalize the rhythmic pulse and incorporate it into the initiation of phrases. Be aware that guitarists play more in the singers' range and can cover up the voice, masking the vocal timbre.

Time feel and phrasing. Some singers orient themselves to the bass line for rhythmic feel and for intonation. Other vocalists key in on the drum, which displays the outer rhythm as well as the subdivision. Isolate each element and respond to the groove to enhance time feel, and phrasing will reflect that. In a trio or RS setting, the instrumentalists are aware and appreciate a singer who interacts with them as a musician rather than regarding them as the rhythm track.

Vocal timbre and inflections. Mellow timbres and smooth attacks from the RS demand corresponding timbres (breathy, medium dynamics, intimate), while edgy, biting attacks and comping from the pianists should have you using accentuated attacks and edgy vocal timbres. Brushes and the acoustic bass imply one set of vocal qualities, while electric bass and sticks imply another. Your vocal timbre should reflect the mood.

Lyric interpretation and style. Whether reading a lead sheet or an arrangement, the instrumentalists create a background on the musical canvas upon which the vocalist paints a scene in a variety of colors and shadings. Don't be ambivalent. Emanate conviction, even if you are forced to take a detour. Tap into a variety of approaches as each member of the group adjusts instrumentation (acoustic to electric, from sticks to brushes, etc.) to develop the material.

Applied voice. As with any instrument fronting an RS, the tone must be assertive, even at soft dynamic levels. In more robust rhythmic feels (shuffles, hip-hop, R & B) ensure that the attack on initial consonants is mediated by breath pulsations rather than by using throat muscles to project the rhythm. Avoid bringing the chin forward and engaging intensity muscles to get your point across.

Rehearsal techniques. Each instrument is autonomous but must be clear with intros and endings as well as climactic points. Everyone must be comfortable with the count-off and be able to articulate verbally and physically the time feel, tempo, and key of the tune.

The Large Performance Arena

The Orchestra: Singing with Strings

> The larger the backup section, the less control, the less freedom as a performer in terms of taking liberties with the melody and length of phrases.
>
> —Julie Silvera-Jensen, personal communication, December 2005

The presence of strings in instrumental accompaniment alters the musical canvas significantly. Phrases become broader with delicate onsets and full-bodied timbres and textures played behind you or heard through studio cans. Sensing the vibrations from the lower strings and double basses can be a spine-tingling experience. Your voice as an instrument should match the warmth and movement of the string section while you are mindful of the rhythmic pulse and movement throughout the orchestra. Recording with string overdubs or synthesized strings does not create the same thrill, but you should still alter the vocal approach to some extent. Strings add warmth and a dimension of melodiousness to instrumental accompaniment, and the introduction of poetry—of words—completes the picture. As soloist in front of an orchestra, you want to convey an attitude that is all-embracing—of making music together. Your energy, attention to detail, and professional demeanor can make the difference between a perfunctory performance with orchestral accompaniment or one that is special, electric.

Preparation: Knowing the Score

As the soloist, you are constrained somewhat by the written, detailed accompaniment that has been rehearsed and (hopefully) polished before your arrival at the rehearsal. Your rehearsal may consist of only one or two full run-throughs. You need to have scoped the arrangement carefully, plotting breaths and phrases, and noted light-textured passages and heavier-textured sections, which will influence your choice of approaches dynamically. If you have been signing predominantly with bands or smaller ensembles without strings, you need to reacquaint yourself to long tapered lines and the sustained focus that singing with an orchestra entails. Even if a song is familiar and frequently performed, reexamining textual nuances and extended vocal lines alters proprioception. Practice the melody as a vocalese, in real time, to build breath support and deliberate releases. If the material is in the musical theatre, operetta, or opera vein, reorienting yourself to vocal projection and rounder, fuller tones and pure vowels requires building up vocal stamina, since you are singing off-mike. You should be vocalizing and running the material daily in order to wear the songs physically as well as interpretively.

Combining the textual elements as phrasing that measures each word and sustaining intensity and interest during instrumental interludes (not letting down between phrases) are crucial. Practicing the song presentation in its entirety and not just in segments prepares you proprioceptively for the real thing, so that once united with the orchestra and the conductor (who will have already imposed an interpretive stamp) you will not be assailed by unfamiliar sensations or become distracted by orchestral matters.

Rehearsal: With Feeling and with the Conductor

Having familiarized yourself with the written score, even if you have heard or performed it before, you should examine the text with the rehearsal numbers to get an idea of the form as well as musical cues. The conductor will probably talk through the arrangement briefly, then run it. You should have a sound recorder running throughout the rehearsal and have a pencil to mark the score or for an aide-mémoire even if you know the score from memory. If you've presented these selections countless times, your confident, secure delivery will win over the ensemble. In some performance situations, the conductor may be visible peripherally, whereas in other performances, you may be up front with the opportunity for stage movement.

Performance: Putting It All Together
As in all performances with large ensembles, tuning in (literally and figuratively) to the rhythmic pulse and the protracted lines is important for cohesion. Be aware of textual changes or pauses that dictate matters of phrasing and vocal presentation and dynamics. It is important to have a definite plan for the treatment of the ending and to communicate it to the conductor and musicians. A polished ending enhances the experience for you, for the orchestra, and for your audience.

Vocal Technique Applications for Singing with Orchestra
   Projection and dynamic range. You need to maintain tone focus and ring for sustained notes to project over strings. Head resonance projects over sustained sonorities. Short utterances need to be sustained and focused.
   Attack and breath management. Use delicate onsets, as strings do. Very broad swelling lines require breath flow in a steady stream, vocal legato, and vibrato present throughout the tone, which facilitates breath support. Because of the long, sustained phrases, identify logical places to breathe when you first start practicing a piece, and mark the music accordingly (with provisional breaths) so that breath habits become internalized as part of phrasing. Inhalation can then be rhythmic.
   Time feel and phrasing. The shrewd vocalist plots sufficient opportunities to inhale, adding to the reservoir of air and never having to take an unrhythmic snatch breath that automatically calls attention to itself. If a breath is rhythmic and makes sense in the context of the words, and the word that follows is buzzed, no one is the wiser. An added dividend is phrasing that sounds inventive but originates out of necessity to camouflage a breath, a trick successful vocalists in all idioms have used for centuries. Due to the nature of written arrangements and the necessity of coordinating a large ensemble, the phrases are

rather self-evident, and phrasing is more a matter of delivering the text in a spontaneous and believable way.

Vocal timbre and inflection. Tone generation and vocal vibrato, which are present throughout, mimic the strings in oscillation. The vocal timbres are closer to classical and musical theatre, with higher tone placement for females.

Lyric interpretation and style. If you compare performances of singers who had the opportunity to sing with both an RS and a studio orchestra, you will note the more sustained resonant treatment with the orchestra. The approach is warm with more crescendos and shaping. Special attention to vocal onset (the term seems more applicable in this context, since initiation of tone is smoother and more gradual than an attack) can draw attention to the text. In addition, deliberate releases with a caressed final consonant represent the polish that also lends to a mesmerizing vocal performance.

Applied voice. Develop the ability to sustain legato. Focus and tone placement permit projection and enhance the voice's unique timbre. Practicing the musical phrases on vowels, like a vocalise, and shaping the phrases with dynamic shadings help develop breath control so you can move the phrase and release comfortably and musically. Then integrate the text, which you will also have practiced separately, for a compelling performance.

Rehearsal techniques. Orchestra music is conductor-centered and composer- or arranger-centered music. You're interpreting a written arrangement, which, to some extent, restricts your interpretive choices. In terms of mechanics, you must be musically secure in entrances and sense the inner pulse as well as the broad instrumental line. Familiarizing yourself thoroughly with the score and with what the individual sections (strings, brass, and woodwinds) are doing is essential because this will affect timbre choices. In rehearsals, time is money, and a full orchestra has limited time for repeat run-throughs. The soloist is expected to be thoroughly prepared and secure, ready to immerse him-/herself in the wonderful experience of singing with a full orchestra.

The Big Band: Singing with Horns
Gigs performing with a big band are becoming few and far between, but some ensembles augmented with a few horns or big band tracks

provide opportunities to sing big band–like arrangements or swing. Switching gears from singing with swelling strings to popping brass illustrates the contrasts in vocal demands as well as representing the diversity of human emotional experience. Because the lead trumpet projects the tone production for the band, your vocals are characterized by crisp articulations into phrases and rhythmic precision including timed releases. The broad, sustained lines of strings are supplanted by sharp, articulated rhythmic figures over the time feel furnished by the rhythm section. Since sound output of a band with horns (or horn tracks) is powerful, the vocal performance must also be rhythmic and intense and assert itself with strength and projection in front of a big band.

Preparation: Navigating the Chart

Unlike an orchestral arrangement, big band arrangements can be challenging to follow, with sections open for solos as well as many repeated sections, second endings, and so on. Rehearsal letters denote numbered measures and sections, and an arrangement resembles a more complicated lead sheet with written horn lines. However, studying the chart, which will have vocal or word cues, feeling the music in bars of 8, 16, 24, 32, and so on, and taking note of distinct sections are critical. A recording of the arrangement facilitates learning it, but making notations as reminders or cues is indispensable. Insecurity at entrances and a tentative sound are antithetical in the big band setting.

Your interpretation is also somewhat dictated by the precise rhythmic figures or background accompaniment of the band. Unlike the walls of sound generated by electronic instruments, brass and reeds breathe, and the arrangements accommodate solo lines by including lighter textures and dynamics. The groove and mood set by the intro set the feeling for vocal approaches. Being aware of the dynamics and textures (flutes and clarinets versus trumpets and 'bones) determines some aspects of the tone quality and delivery. Familiarize yourself with those features of the chart to influence your performance.

Rehearsal

As with the orchestral gig, you will be expected to know the arrangement and be able to present it on the first run-through like other professional musicians. Jazz band players are famous for being quick readers, and vocal charts are usually simple when compared to instrumental features. In a large theatre where a jazz band might play, your delivery must be assertive, rhythmic, and powerful to justify your fronting the band or you will be overwhelmed. Style through glitches as though your interpretation was intentional, translating the instrumental energy into an aggressive attitude. You should communicate the lyrics and mood immediately. Record the rehearsal for review later, and mark your chart to deflect any insecurity. Having a music stand slightly to the side is not unheard of, particularly for complicated arrangements, but performing minus the chart is more powerful and earns you the respect of the band.

Performance: Banding Together

Letting the tongue (particularly the tip of the tongue) do the work in enunciation contributes to clarity and emphasis, particularly on microphone. Use inflections and embellishments to style and tap into the high range (even head voice tone but brighter) to build intensity. Since you're interpreting the chart, choreograph your big notes for heavier textures and relax in lighter textures for pacing. Be sure to prepare an approach to the last chorus and ending, whether it be the lingering, warm release for a ballad or a big or high note for a livelier number. Either way, you should have a final say, along with the band.

Vocal Technique Applications Singing with Horns

> I'd rather play with a drummer than with a conductor.
>
> —Alexander Pope Norris, personal communication,
> December 4, 2005

Projection and dynamic range. You must overcome brass, at full blast, at times. This demands an aggressive approach to punctuate and complement the instrumental lines. Be aware of textures and dynamics in the arrangement that dictate vocal delivery. Lighter textures (reeds, background pads) allow for pacing within the arrangement. In shout choruses, you can wail in head-voice to project screech vocals, singing in unison with the lead trumpet line.

Attack and breath management. You must complement crisp attacks of brass with aggressive, punctuated articulations into phrases. Coordination with the breath and vocal flexibility must be optimal. Releases must also be rhythmic and precise.

Time feel and phrasing. For singing with a jazz band, playing to the RS and the rhythm and subdivision are crucial. Your releases must be very rhythmic and integral with the time, particularly in swing, and you must treat phrasing accordingly. In up-tempo arrangements, keep phrases clipped, with deliberate releases, like rhythmic figures, and use variety in length. Allow phrasing to accommodate the time feel, rather than vice versa. In jazz, time feel is a priority, and precision translates into energy.

Vocal timbre and inflection. Vocal edge and "oomph" are required for aggressive passages. Just as arrangers write in articulations, markings that instruct the trumpets how to tongue into the notes, you have to display the same attack and assertive approach. Use embellishments such as slurs, flips, and percussive initial consonants to emphasize important words and phrases. Ballads also incorporate runs, embellishments, and improvised lines at dynamic levels that project outward even as they convey intimacy.

Lyric interpretation and style. Look for clarity in enunciation, and choreograph the words by the way you pronounce them. Each word is approached with deliberate emphasis. Sustained vowels should crescendo until the release. You must maintain a large, strong presence so as not to be overwhelmed by the band.

Applied voice. Your voice must assert itself. Develop vocal flexibility and agility, like coloratura. Make sure that you coordinate aggressive vocal initiation, disengaging the neck and throat muscles and maintaining strength in the midsection. Maximize the assistance of the microphone to project.

Rehearsal technique. Whether you are a reader or not, instrumentalists will not wait for vocalists to learn music, particularly jazz bands, whose members are excellent sight readers. Rehearsals usually consist of run-throughs and refining, because vocal arrangements are generally comparatively straight-ahead and uncomplicated as compared to instrumental features. Band music is calculated in defined sections, broken down into 8-bar phrases represented by rehearsal letters, with long solos. Familiarize yourself with the form, know your entrances, and be secure in your delivery. Taping the rehearsal to help you internalize the form, textures, and dynamics of the arrangement is a smart move. Standing before a big band requires a powerful, assertive delivery rhythmically and musically.

Rock and Blues Bands: Singing with Electric Guitars

The introduction of electricity imposed more pressure on vocalists to project, without becoming vocally electri-fried. The human vocal mechanism is limited when competing with electricity because instruments only need to boost a channel or adjust a knob on the amp to bring up the volume. With instruments maxed when the mike levels are set, concern about feedback arises. Strategies to cope with sound reinforcement include

- Having a good sound check with comfortable levels and equalization.
- Having your own individual monitor.
- Being pleasant and cooperative with the sound engineer.
- Using effects such as reverb, digital delay, and other enhancements, which can take the load (literally) off the vocal folds.

Preparation: Generating Intensity without Vocal Sacrifice
Don't waste voice tweaking issues of form, instrumentation, and so on. Practice on a microphone away from the band to calibrate output versus effort. Much of the visible effort in high-energy performing is illusion by skilled performers. Inflection, exaggerated consonants, edgy vowels, and prolonging sibilants (*s, t, sh,* and other digraphs, etc.) with the high-spectral energy facilitates clarity.

Practice projecting the words with authority aloud, then with modulation, then finally adding a melody. You can then measure effort in the context of the instrumentation even if you can't monitor yourself optimally in performance. Proprioceptive memory could help avoid straining, as could using ear monitors if available. Some singers find using a single ear plug useful for self-monitoring, and this can also filter out excessively loud ambient instrumental noise.

Rehearsal: Save Voice, Save Time

Don't waste voice on run-throughs intended to deal with form and instrumental issues. Save your maximum output for the final few go-rounds so that you're not fried after rehearsal. Gradually build endurance by introducing more vocalization when polishing. Use a monitor in rehearsals and verify that keys allow you to tap into your power notes comfortably. Rock artists with enduring careers are cognizant of the importance of a lifestyle that enables them to cope with the rigors of athletically and vocally demanding schedules. A sound engineer at rehearsals is a smart investment that helps you preserve your voice and prevent missed performances due to vocal dysfunction. Engineers can also contribute to consistent sound production in different environments, requiring less adjustment from the singers.

Performance: Optimal Vocal Production and Pacing

Pacing within a song (low-intensity levels) and programming instrumentals and quiet, acoustic ballads help achieve good pacing. Maintaining an upright position, staying loose at the joints, particularly at the knees, is crucial. Head mikes make it easier to keep the chin level, but if you are standing, position the mike stand so that the chin is level and the body is comfortable, and disengage the muscles in the neck and shoulders.

Be attuned to your vocal and physical condition and incorporate substitutions to accommodate less than ideal performance situations. As in any athletic endeavor, activities that stretch the limits of the body entail warming up, pacing, cooling down, and conditioning, or the risk for injury is higher. The professional rehearses intelligently so that the body, mind, and voice are in their optimal condition for performance.

Vocal Technique Applications Singing with Rock and Blues Bands

> When you're out in front of a rock band or a blues band you have to really root yourself to the stage, and your whole body is involved, you're bending at the knees and at the waist, but your chin is tucked. It sounds tight but your body can't be tense.
>
> —Wendy Pedersen, personal communication, 2005

Projection. You are competing with electricity, so you have to maximize output. You can't fight physiology, regardless of your vocal strength, so your ability to compete with the volume levels of others in the band is limited. Know when you have maxed out and don't sacrifice voice. Using sibilants and other high-spectral energy can help you project as a distinguishable timbre with clarity and energy while enhancing lyric communication. You can make use of effects (reverb, digital delay, etc.) to match instruments and aid projection. A dry sound minus reverberation or continuation of sound tends to exact more laryngeal involvement, since, as opposed to reverberation, the tone begins and ends with vocal fold vibration. The effects are more intense for the female voice than the male voice (more muscle means more fullness at the sound source).

Attack and breath management. Use speech or shout-like qualities with popped, crisp consonants and emphatic delivery. Maintain freedom in the upper body and use the midsection to pulsate and the lower body to support independently to maximize output without straining.

Time feel and phrasing. Use detached and speech-like utterances. You should practice projected speech first before adding the music. Practice with a quarter- or eighth-note pulse for rock and blues, or sixteenths for funk. Your phrasing must broadcast the pulse.

Vocal timbre and inflections. Use growls and extra-vocal sounds liberally. Your voice can display attitude, such as snarling, sneering, angry, and so on, but is usually aggressive. Edgy vowels are predominant. You must condition the voice and work on maintaining vocal endurance. Sophisticated sound design and the addition of devices can create the illusion of effort that is abetted by mixing at the sound board. It's not a bad investment to engage a professional engineer, which may not save you money but can save your voice. Key choices are particularly important, especially for females. Since rock idioms entail considerable vocal energy, technique must be optimal, with no lifted chin or uncoordinated attacks. Vocal hygiene must be optimal as well.

Lyric interpretation and style. Individualize vocal approach. The moment you stand before a rock band, you must assume a large presence, with an individualized personal style. In rock, theatrics are intertwined with presentation in combination with movement, reinforcing the need to have a flexible upper body. Awareness of pacing is important. Words underscored by exaggerated inflections and attitude reflect extreme emotion. Vocal expression trumps vocal quality.

Applied voice. Coming full circle, reinforced vocalism now confronts exigencies for projection over loud accompaniment. Maximize consonant and vowel projection (e.g., using the tip of the tongue to direct the sound into the microphone). Avoid lifting the chin and other postural anomalies that obstruct your sound output. Exploit the vocal edge and ring in the sound and learn to maximize the effectiveness of reinforced sound.

Rehearsals. Pacing is the key to vocal maintenance. Don't waste voice by rehearsing insecure sections in full voice. Your body will tighten due to being insecure musically. Run through musical stumbling blocks first, marking until you begin to work on execution. Work yourself up gradually. As with any athletic endeavor, warming up and cooling down are essential, as are pacing and building up your endurance. Don't fully resume singing after laying out for a significant length of time. Gradually pace your return into the full program. Judicious use of an instrument that is used at high-intensity levels for an extended time demands optimal preparation and execution.

~

CHAPTER THREE

Crossing Over from Microphone Idioms to Classical Idioms

The Acoustic Arena

The orchestra seems behind the conductor's beat because the strings naturally respond late. With a band or hybrid (studio orchestra), go with the rhythm section.

—Chris O'Farrill, personal communication, December 13, 2005

The boundaries between vocal idioms are becoming increasingly blurred as vocalists are exploring the worlds of classical, rock, soul, gospel, folk, and world music, both acoustic and reinforced. I have had the privilege to work with individuals who have had careers in microphone idioms and wished to explore vocalism in the classical, world music, and acoustic realms. Their objectives may have stemmed from a desire to sing their favorite arias, to participate in a traditional choral ensemble, to be able to produce a traditional choral sound on demand in the recording studio, or to sing free from the need for electrical inputs. A few may have wished to revisit classical voice study after abandoning it to pursue their business careers. Like their classical counterparts, these microphone singers wish to explore alternative musical idioms. The commonality in both streams is a genuine desire to sing and explore the voice, the enjoyment of great literature, and an enthusiasm for new sensations and sounds while communicating human emotion.

How Do Instrumentalists Adjust to Microphone Idioms?

The observations by brass and reed players who routinely alternate between classical performance and commercial or jazz idioms were informative and revealing. In responding to an inquiry concerning adjustments made in crossing over, both a trumpet player and saxophone player emphasized that, in the classical realm, achievement of a target tone quality was the paramount objective. Orchestra trumpet player Chris O'Farrill (as well as arranger and lead trumpeter for a number of big bands, including Woody Herman's) mentioned that classical trumpet players were even "pigeonholed by their timbre" (Personal communication, December 13, 2005), Both instrumentalists changed their mouthpiece to achieve the desired sound for each idiom. According to Gary Keller, professor of saxophone in the Studio Music and Jazz Program at the University of Miami,

> For classical playing I do change to a mouthpiece that gives a darker, more consistent tone and is easier to control in the extreme registers and at softer volumes—jazz mouthpieces sacrifice some of this control for the added volume and brilliance and potential for a broader tonal palette. (Personal communication, June 6, 2005)

Alas, changing mouthpieces is not an option for vocalists, but it underscores the importance placed on an objectified tone quality and tone production in traditional idioms for instrumentalists as well as singers.

Traditional or classical singing parallels this orientation toward an objectified vocal sound by virtue of the vocal range, voice categorization, and phrasing characteristics specified by the music as composed. However, adjusting the vocal tract through coupling of the resonators and articulators and the management of breath and airflow are among the changes that confront the vocalist crossing over.

Adaptations to Acoustic Vocal Performance

Following an intense schedule of microphone singing exclusively, the major issues inherent in switching to acoustic idioms include the following:

Power generation. While your counterpart switching from acoustic singing to microphone singing learns to allow the microphone to assist in projection, you must remember that, in singing acoustically, all breath management and power generation for projection must come from you! That is an eye-opener and underscores how the effective use of sound reinforcement can aid in projecting and pacing. Acoustically, minute tonal shadings and nuances do not travel to the listener's ear and are lost. Ironically, classical performers are increasingly making use of sound reinforcement in singing classical works, which removes some of the burden on vocal projection.

Monitoring acoustically. Monitoring yourself in the hall or room rather than from the sound speakers is an ear-opener. This challenge entails considerable adjustment and can lead to insecurity. The inability to hear yourself and respond to the vocal sound being fed back to you can be disconcerting when you are conditioned to monitoring yourself reinforced.

Singing legato. Long, legato phrases demand adjustments in breath flow and management for sustained phonation. The vocal sound must be resonant and focused to travel to the listener in the last row. Since the phrases are more prolonged, they permit you to make discrete adjustments in tone focus while sustaining the tone, an option not available in idioms in which the sounds are rapid and florid.

Using vibrato. Using vibrato throughout the tone facilitates vocal legato as well as connection with the breath stream. The rate and pitch modulation of the vibrato feel excessive initially and lacking in sufficient pitch center on high notes. This also can make a commercial or jazz vocalist feel insecure after being exposed to derisive comments regarding classical vibrato from band members at professional gigs. One antidote is to mimic the vibrato used by the strings.

Vocal attack or vocal onset. The use of what the trumpet player described as a "delicate onset" and singing through consonants assist in attaining a flowing vocal line. This contrasts sharply to the various inflections and articulations into phrases in microphone idioms. You shouldn't try to pinpoint a pitch, but introduce vocal vibrato immediately as part of the vocal onset.

Tone focus. The light, bright falsetto that I use for high notes in jazz or pop won't work here. Rather, placing the tone with higher vertical focus and head resonance helps me avoid sounding pinched. The tone needs to be fuller and rounder, achieved through the arched palate and maintenance of the relaxed jaw. This entails some modification initially, and the singer can feel "hooty" in comparison to the brighter qualities used in commercial idioms. For male singers, tapping into a ring and the top voice can be daunting, but achievable. Ultimately, the kinesthetic adjustments are more distinct for the female voice.

Tongue placement. The tip of my tongue remains more stationary than in declamatory styles, with the tip forward but not pushing against the lower teeth. Regional accents and idiosyncratic characteristics (with the associated tensions) may lend themselves to a unique sound in microphone idioms but contribute to tension and are not conducive to vocal freedom in the higher vocal range. Vowel modification in the higher ranges can feel artificial, but recording the voice can provide reassurance.

Singing in foreign languages. This presents an additional challenge. Talented vocalists possess the ear to be able to imitate and should use oral practice to achieve relative fluency while singing. In the words of Jon Eisenson (1985),

> Adults who wish to learn a second dialect, to change from one regional to another, or to become bidialectal must be willing to immerse themselves in the effort. . . . To a degree, it is much like learning a second language. It will not be achieved by silent study or even by careful listening, though both will help. Learning a new dialect, or modifying a dialect influence, requires a willingness to hear ourselves as others hear us, and to practice orally as well as aurally whatever needs to be practiced to modify our linguistic habits in the direction of a desired goal.

Movement and deflection of nervous energy through dance movement. This is available in microphone idioms, but motion is limited in traditional genres, unless the piece is choreographed. You have to be comfortable in your own skin, with feet firmly planted, without appearing stiff, which can constitute a major challenge, particularly in dealing with the hands. Subtle (unobtrusive) changes in position during musical interludes can help initially.

Building vocal stamina. In commercial idioms, I can pace myself somewhat by taking detours in a song since I have the flexibility to interpolate notes and tailor phrasing to my breath capacity and vocal condition. In classical singing, you must develop considerable vocal and physical stamina to cope with the long vocal lines, extreme ranges, and dynamics demanded. Considerable physical control is exacted to conform to accompaniments written for large ensembles. Expectations represent an additional pressure in a literal medium. The programmed high C at the end is known to everyone, and singer and audience anxiously wait in anticipation.

Choral blend. Within the context of the choral ensemble, the adjustments, particularly for the inner parts, are less radical but entail reduction of edge or harshness that could penetrate and compromise choral blend.

Strategies in Crossing Over Effectively to the Classical World

Find a favorite music selection. Gravitate toward music that appeals to you and that mirrors the voice mode that seems appropriate to express the emotion, the text, or the circumstances.

Listen. Just as listening in microphone idioms can be instructive and inspiring, it is even more applicable in this context, owing to the nature of classical music as a literal, composer-centered medium. Exposure to various renditions of "Quando m'en vo" or "Deh vieni alla finestra" can help place the music and the language in your ear and your memory, easing the way into performance.

Vocal exercises. Classical vocal exercises and books are plentiful. Some singers embrace them while others prefer exercises formulated from excerpts extracted from the music being studied. Whatever the style of learning, try them! Vocalises and vocal exercises contribute to voice building, allowing the voice to become a responsive instrument, ready for the musical task.

Isolate elements. Independent study of the music on vowels and speaking the text in rhythm with expression are effective in this context as well. Once the song is assembled, kinesthetic memory can take over.

Imitate. A favorite anecdote of my voice teacher applies here. A young mezzo's breakthrough lesson came when, frustrated, she sarcastically imitated a famous mezzo, saying, "Oh, you want me to sound like her!—like this!" To which the teacher replied, "Yes! That's it!" Eventually, the student became less sarcastic and landed roles with the Houston Grand Opera.

Phrasing as written. Treating vocal lines as if you were designing the phrasing yourself (albeit more extended versions than the more condensed, short phrases in popular styles) can help you achieve a sense of line and coordinate breath support. Deferring to the prosody of the language being sung is crucial. Breathing with feeling as part of the rhythmic pulse allows the breath and phrasing to coalesce from vocal onset to release, contributing to the arc and motion.

Contouring. Sing the general shape of the vocal line on a vowel, with feeling, maintaining vibrato throughout. Use this as a step between reciting the text in rhythm and uniting the vocal line with the text.

Expressive enunciation. Sensuality and emotion in any language are characterized by attention to and investment in each utterance. From the audience perspective, "if we listen to what is spoken slowly and are able to maintain attention while listening, we assume that what we have heard is more important than more quickly spoken content" (Eisenson 1985). Therefore deliberateness in delivery effects how a text is perceived. Ultimately, tasting the language while singing, relishing how it feels, can help us overcome the foreign sensations that can intimidate us when we present a piece in an unfamiliar language. Sing sensually.

Sing operetta and traditional musical theatre. Using traditional, soubrette role selections ("Till There Was You," "You'll Never Walk Alone") or songs for the more full-voiced male roles can function as a bridge from microphone idioms to a more classical sound. The fact that the voice quality is embodied in characterization can help make classical technique more accessible. For microphone idioms and musical theatre, your vocal sound is the means to an end and not the final objective. Tracing vocal production through the characterization and implicit emotion can direct you to the appropriate vocal technique.

Study with a classical pedagogue. Choose someone who appreciates versatility and will work with you in exploring classical vocal literature.

CHAPTER FOUR

Pedagogical Approaches to Microphone Idioms

Teaching with Sound Reinforcement

Unlike the student of classical music (and, to an extent, the jazz vocalist) the aspiring commercial or popular musician is not a tabula rasa, devoid of any exposure to the popular musical idioms. Likely he/she already imitates a few favorite artists, writes original material, plays guitar or piano, and can produce (or find someone to record and produce) a CD in the home studio. Students tend to have a point of view—a perspective and a sense, though somewhat vague and ever-changing, regarding vocal identity and creative direction. Many tend to be independent with a desire to maintain custody of their own talent. As a result, the voice teacher serves more as a coach, guiding the singer toward the performance objective. The pedagogical approach of throwing everything out and starting from scratch could be counterproductive for this type of student.

"Singers tend to be affective speakers," as speech pathologist Vivian Topp asserts (Personal communication, June 2005), and they can tend to be affective singers as well, focusing on the intuitive rather than the analytical. There is a point at which the cerebral, analytical singer has to let go, or the result is a flat performance. Teaching toward a specific vocal quality overlooks an individual singer's musical growth, the ever-changing vocal mechanism, and the evocation of differing emotional states. Young singers often take detours to uncover new directions and avenues for growth, including classical or traditional idioms, becoming the richer when they return "home"—closer to achieving their own sound. In commercial idioms, singers treasure individuality of sound and perspective as they seek to assert their own voice. The commercial vocal pedagogue works with the individual instrument and teaches within the context of the music the singer aspires to perform. This enables the vocal musician to have an understanding of and exert control over the instrument, gaining insight while on the road to accomplishing career objectives musically, expressively, and with longevity and endurance.

Vocal Technique on Microphone

Exercises and repertoire should be performed on microphone early in the process of learning a song. This allows vocalists to

- Become comfortable at hearing themselves through sound speakers.
- Gauge dynamic levels vis-à-vis vocal effort.
- Adjust microphone response to varying oral and lingual positions for oral resonance.
- Experiment with treatment of consonants and pronunciation on the microphone.
- Determine comfortable tessitura and selection of key.

The following exercises can be performed on the microphone:

- Use the *messa di voce* on microphone on vowels in conjunction with words (e.g., *love, me, you, say, so, last*). Experiment with tongue placement. The tip of the tongue does not remain stationary and can be more flexible and active in the speaking range, particularly since most utterances are short.
- Say the words of the text in rhythm (particularly high-energy tunes) to maximize projection using efficient vocal function. A cheat sheet consisting of words set down as a poem that is easily readable from a music stand to the side should be available at the outset.

- Sing the melody of the song on vowels like a vocalise, articulating the breath flow, pulsing for shaping the phrase.
- Assemble lyrics and melody at a comfortable medium dynamic level. Depending on your preference and ease, a ballad or patter tune is useful in this context. At this juncture, the memorization process should be complete, save for a few occasional peeks at the lyric.
- Finally, add the piano accompaniment or rhythm track. By this time you should have internalized the tune and the text.

By practicing on mike, the singer learns how to achieve vocal intensity, dynamic control, equalization of the voice, and microphone projection prior to performance. The sound output on mike (which would sound comparatively moderate acoustically) projects effectively, and singers report it feels almost casual once coordinated. Overexertion inevitably results if the vocalist tries to adjust to the sound while singing off mike.

Male vocalists croon in some understated styles, while flaunting full voice in the high register (occasionally adding roughness to the vocal sound) for certain performance situations or musical idioms. For many male singers, it seems to be a point of honor to sing in the original key, and they may steadfastly resist transposing downward if the original key is too high. It requires some convincing (and taping) to persuade them that the vocal sound is just as robust (if not more so) when the key correlates with the naturally intense areas of the voice. The classical ring and projection do not suggest baritone, but rather "bari/tenor," with considerable pulsing, as opposed to legato with continuous vibrato. The sound is lighter for ballads, but with inflection or articulation on each note. The adaptations for males in crossing over are less stringent, since they generally sing within the same register in both idioms. However, they do tap into falsetto to a much greater degree and incorporate inflections that, along with phrasing, contribute to a more commercial sound.

Voice Mode

Colloquial Speech Production

Colloquial speech, in the modal or speaking range, goes hand in hand with achieving a sound that seems natural and uncontrived. Speaking voice does not automatically imply chest voice. A healthy speech pattern with optimal pitch levels and good vertical and horizontal placement entails balanced muscular action without undue effort. This is also why an understanding of healthy speech patterns is essential. In idioms that are closely allied to colloquial speech, abusive speech habits and deleterious patterns might more vividly be brought to the attention of the student by a speech pathologist, particularly if the singer experiences an episode of vocal fatigue or vocal dysfunction. In my experience, the dangers of hard onset, poor vocal hygiene, and reckless lifestyle habits are underscored when explained in the vocabulary and with the expertise of a professional voice therapist. Commercial/popular singers tend to make technical adjustments and use vocal exercises when they are persuaded that they are not sacrificing their sound by singing more efficiently. Following spoken text and vowel exercises, the singer exerts more vocal control with freedom to interpret.

Registration: Singing in the Speaking Range

> Probably a very important difference between normal speech and singing is that in normal speech the passive expiratory recoil forces of the breathing apparatus habitually tend to play a more important role in establishing the needed subglottic pressure, while in singing active muscle forces are more important.

> —Johann Sundberg, *The Science of the Singing Voice*

In low-intensity tunes (ballads, bossa novas, narrative tunes), use the breath pressure employed in coordinated speech as a point of departure. Don't oversupport for low notes at a low dynamic. For vocalization at low pitches, the vocal folds should be flaccid, offering little resistance to the breath, producing a tone that is full and warm (and the mike will pick it up). In normal, conversational speech, we do not overinhale as if we know precisely what we plan to say or how we are going to express it. Rather, we breathe and pause to replenish as we search for words and organize our thoughts. Oversupporting causes the vocal folds to become taut, reducing thickness and resulting in a thinner quality, requiring us to work harder for subsequent passages at higher intensity. Singing is always on the breath, but maintaining breath pressure and proportional support at low intensity (generally at the beginning of the song) enables us to adjust breath support and projection as the melody ascends and the demand for more intensity and projection increases.

Building Intensity and Agility

> The feeling of suppleness in fast-moving passages is akin to the umbilical-epigastric movement experienced in rapid silent panting. This movement in the anterior abdominal wall resembles quick staccato onset activity, incorporated, however, into the articulated legato.
>
> —Richard Miller, *The Structure of Singing*

In singing at high-intensity levels, conversely, and with instrumental accompaniment characterized by crisp articulations with bite courtesy of horns and electric guitars, the breath is used in pulsation, a kind of "articulated legato" (R. Miller 1986). In classical genres, achieving a seamless legato implies the expiration of a steady stream of air, which engages the lower abdominal muscles for sustained phonation. In rapid passages, or passages requiring agility, pulsation is sensed a bit higher, directly below the sternum, with the support sensed in the inspiratory muscles of the ribs laterally. According to Greene and Mathieson, "stressed syllables require an increase in subglottic pressure obtained by the intercostal muscles, whereas in connected speech, the abdominal muscles contribute to the control of respiration" (1989).

The distinction is a salient one. In rapid utterances, pulsation originating from the lower abdominal muscles, with less checking or inhibitory action by the intercostals, results in a diffuse stream of air that blows over the vocal folds, with less focus. Conversely, pulsating from the diaphragm, or more accurately, the "bouncing epigastrium" (as William Vennard [1967] calls it), or what Richard Miller calls "umbilical-epigastric control" (1986), engages the external intercostals as well, with the attendant resistance resulting in the expiration of a pulse of air that is more concentrated and more efficient. Once the student relates to that area, avoiding the "slumping sternum" (R. Miller 1986) for rapid passages, agility and flexibility improve perceptibly. An added dividend is that centering in the area below the sternum encourages body extension and frees the upper body for any choreography or stage movement. For dancers, who are accustomed to overextension, centering slightly lower than they are accustomed to frees the upper body, but they can still feel that they are extending.

Dealing with Climactic Notes and Passages

> Covering incurs fundamental changes in the mechanical function of the larynx and alteration of the shape of the resonators, with the accommodation of additional spaciousness in the pharynx, a high velum, a low tongue and lowered larynx.
>
> —Richard Miller, *The Structure of Singing*

The C^5 sung at the climactic point of the tune for a female shares some characteristics with a tenor's high C as he hooks into it, sometimes adding a kind of flip or yodel to the note. Some pop and country singers use the same approach. The concomitant effects include an arched palate and a low larynx, balancing the CT (cricothyroid) and TA (thyroarytenoid) muscles.

In climactic passages with amplification, if the voice is equalized, it can have a spoken quality and can be robust but need not be chest voice or "heavy mechanism" (an alternate term for chest voice or pushing used by Vennard [1967]) nor heavily *mechanized*. According to Sundberg (1993), the illusion of depth or volume of sound is provided by the expanded rib cage. Ultimately, vocal extensity, which refers to the depth or fullness of sound, is also dependent on maintaining the connection with the lower body, even at very soft dynamic levels (Lebon 1999). The question of whether the result is chest voice or a mixed voice becomes immaterial, as the vocal quality sets the energy, dynamics, and attitude of the passage being sung. Jazz vocalist and pedagogue Sunny Wilkinson observes,

> There is indeed a misconception that in order to sing pop or jazz—you automatically take the chest mix up high into the range. That just isn't true. There are several kinds of pop singing, and in my opinion, it is the teacher's responsibility to teach different approaches to the mix. We certainly teach this in classical music. Adjusting the mix depends on tessitura and phrasing. (Spradling 2000)

According to LoVetri (2003), "Musical theater requires singers to be as versatile as possible and often asks women to sing in chest, mixed (chest and head) and a 'legit' head within the same show and sometimes within the same song. In order to do this safely, without injury, it is absolutely necessary that women learn to feel specifically what 'weight' means in their sound, and learn to make the sound have a spoken (modal) quality without extra pressure in the throat itself."

Contrary to some pedagogical points of view, I do not consider the high larynx the sine qua non of belting or vigorous vocalism. The larynx may be higher than it is for singing classical literature (as some research has suggested), but to sing with that objective can induce tension and limit variety in vocal qualities. Rather, the arched palate and low but flexible tongue serve to counteract constriction with pharyngeal space, enabling the singer to make nuanced adjustments to control timbres on microphone. Experienced belters and R & B vocalists have often described the proprioceptive sensation of peak notes within a phrase or vocal line as an "up and over" sensation, as opposed to the physical tendency to lift the chin or shorten the posterior neck muscles. According to Titze, "there are clear differences in the laryngeal muscle activity between open and covered (or register-mixed) singing. The differences seem to suggest a more economic and efficient use of muscular effort in covered singing" (2002). Idyllically, vocal coloration, a variety of vocal timbres and even character voices can be accomplished by allowing the microphone to create the illusion of depth or largeness of sound rather than enlisting undue vocal effort.

Resonance: Acquiring Edge in Modal Register

Edge is to commercial idioms as ring is to classical. It is the high-frequency energy and focus that allow vocal quality to assert itself over competing sonorities. The vertical focus tends to hover around the ethmoid sinuses rather than the frontal sinuses. The horizontal focus is sensed as a snarl or whine, which should be balanced by the arched palate. When edge is combined with a relaxed jaw, facilitating oral resonance that directs the vocal energy to the microphone, the result is a depth and richness of the vocal timbre achieved through optimal tone focus rather than from the throat.

It's important to rehearse on microphone to identify sounds that will travel on mike that would not ordinarily work acoustically, particularly if you are competing with amplified instrumentation. Exercises combining nasal glides followed by consonants that increase pharyngeal space or lower the tongue (ŋga) facilitate achieving focus while maintaining an open throat.

The Issue of Vibrato

> Next comes the issues of the decay of the note, and the inevitable vibrato. Try to get a classical violinist not to vibrato . . . just try! Vibrato, I think, should only appear near the end of an articulated note, and should normally be a slower oscillation than a typical violin vibrato.
>
> —Glenn Basham, personal communication, July 2005

In everyday speech, we do not speak with vibrato throughout the tone, since our utterances are not sustained. In singing that mimics spoken conversation, with clipped phrasing, consistent vibrato would be obtrusive. In commercial/jazz idioms, when vibrato is used, it appears on extended notes at the ends of phrases to achieve a graceful release. If the vocalist is coordinated, vibrato manifests itself naturally. Some singers use a short twist vibrato at the very end of the utterance. Others wind it up with straight tone dissolving into vibrato.

In the straight-tone singing found in some idioms, attention is still paid to the release, which is with the breath. Some idioms derivative of gospel use embellishments and inflections as part of the attack as well as the release, following the vibrato. The most obvious (and annoying) indication that a singer has a classical orientation is the ever-present prominent vibrato, which is always regarded as excessive if it is injected into the tone rather than being an offshoot of the release or inflection. Regardless of the vocal style or the manner in which vibrato manifests itself, singing that is coordinated with the breath demonstrates versatility and exhibits a variety of uses of vibrato depending on the particular song and style being presented.

Phrasing and Lyric Interpretation Displaying Spontaneity

The aural–oral nature of commercial/jazz idioms dictates that it is up to the vocalist to render the mood and emotions and bring meaning to the lyrics independently, creatively, and spontaneously within the rhythmic groove set by the band. The implication is that the singer needs to have formulated a mood, a point of view surrounding the song lyrics that is reflected in the phrasing, and by extension, the vocal quality. Certain method actor singers can intuitively connect quickly and emotionally. Others should isolate the words and recite the poetry inherent in the lyrics as soon as they begin to learn a song so that the meaning of the text and the rhythm of the language become familiar early in the learning process. Singers who learn the song reading the music tend to subordinate the lyrics to the rhythm of the music as printed. Strategies that generate spontaneity in phrasing include

- Playing traffic cop, forcing the student to delay entrances, resulting in tension and rhythmic interest.
- Emphasizing microphrasing. In well-crafted songs, words are not wasted. Each word has import, and just as we think in fragments, we deliver words that have weight with emphasis, however subtle. Have the singer choreograph critical words by enunciation, inflection, or tone quality, treating the word differently each time.
- Encouraging the suspended vocal line with pauses (important in effective phrasing), and by the way short phrases are released. Carmen McCrae and Shirley Horn are particularly adept at maintaining interest and anticipation through pauses.
- Pointing out that actors create a story or subtext behind a song, creating a scenario that generates the approach to words and phrases. Adjusting the background story and generalized emotion or mood (disappointment, anger, sarcasm) furnishes a new perspective on a tired tune (Lebon 1999).

Interaction with Instrumental Accompaniment without Intimidation

He [the popular singer] calculates his rhythmic progress in terms of four- or eight-measure episodes rather than in terms of so many beats to the measure, subdivided arithmetically, as in classical music. Within these four- or eight-measure episodes he distributes syllables at his own oratorical and rhetorical discretion, taking a bit of time from one, giving it to another.

—Henry Pleasants, *The Great American Popular Singers*

Singers are often regarded as second-rate musicians or divas because they can tend to focus on their vocal performance rather than on the bigger musical picture. However, for vocalists who are also musicians, the music does not begin when they open their mouth and end when they stop singing, regardless of musical style or genre. They tend to display awareness and involvement in the instrumental introduction and the musical ambiance as the stage is set.

Just as projection and breadth of performance are different if a classical vocalist sings with a full orchestra or with a piano accompanist, the nature of instrumentation influences the timbres, dynamics, and inflections of the vocalist in microphone idioms as well. When a vocalist sings with the sustained lines and delicate articulations of string accompaniment, the vocal onsets into words and phrases and how they are sustained (degree of vibrato, tapered phrases) tend to correspond. In contrast, when singing with brass sections, with the tongued articulations of horns, singers tend to respond with articulated inflections into words and phrases to project and maintain intensity. Electric guitars, synthesizers, and sequencers require singers to project more to assert the vocal timbre over electricity, and the overall presentation tends to be more expansive to balance the increased instrumental output. There is a corresponding largeness of delivery and presentation, not unlike the adjustment imposed on an actor going from subtle on-camera acting to a live stage performance. Whether the accompaniment sets a rhythmic groove that the vocalist complements and phrases around or the phrasing accommodates a preset written accompaniment, the rhythmic interaction and mutual response to the rhythmic pulse contribute to an integrated musical performance.

Rehearsals
The opportunity to rehearse on microphone with the complete instrumental accompaniment is not often available, although with home studios, band in a box MIDI, the Internet, and prerecorded tracks with adjustable keys are making it easier to achieve some semblance of an actual performance situation. If you are dealing with piano only, it is essential that the keyboard player *not play the melody notes*, which is not the case with literal idioms. Even in musical theatre, the pianist should

refrain from playing the melody, since it is constraining to the vocalist in terms of phrasing.

Microphone Singing Following
Intensive Classical Singing

Some expressions and terminology related to the commercial/jazz repertoire are "popping for a belting and driving song, pulsing the energy rather than the linear line for ballads, or using a more spontaneous, 'in the moment' breath—lyrics are the vehicle for the music" (Sheila Marchant Barish, personal communication, April 2005). After a heavy schedule of church solos or recitals, you might make the following adjustments when reorienting to singing on the microphone:

Resonance and tone focus. On microphone, reorient tone focus toward middle voice placement, in addition to the oral resonance that microphone amplification affords. After using head voice resonance predominantly in classical singing, you're inclined to revert to a higher vertical placement reflexively, with more air flow.

Phrasing and interpretation. Compress and punctuate phrases. The attack or articulation (jazz) is more punctuated in initiating phrases. Because phrasing is more compressed, you don't have time to adjust resonance and intonation since utterance is not elongated.

Vibrato. Vibrato can become obtrusive and get out of line if tone focus in the middle and lower ranges is placed too high. For example, if tone focus when sustaining the E♭ above middle C (E♭4) is sensed as concentrated in the forehead (frontal sinuses) area as opposed to the between the eyes, around the bridge of the nose (ethmoid sinuses), the vibrato tends to be obtrusive and can compromise intonation.

Breath management. Articulate breath pulses in aggressive styles, as opposed to legato. Use more tonguing or crisp articulations like a trumpet rather than being delicate like strings. Relax breath pressure in the low to middle speaking range to increase support and breath pressure in ascending passages that build to a climax. This is critical, for there is an inclination to overinhale as if you are preparing to sing a long, legato line with continuous airflow. In medium-dynamic ballads or up-tempo tunes with comparatively short phrases, the inhalation need not be much more than in speech, provided that you initiate each utterance with the breath, whether it begins with a consonant or a vowel. As the old adage says, you breathe to sing and not sing to breathe. An inspiratory breath that is out of proportion with the phrase induces tension in the body and is an impediment to controlling dynamics as well.

Microphone. Remember to monitor from the speakers, and allow the microphone to furnish projection. If your breath is not coordinated, you can overcorrect the overinhalation, and your breath becomes shallow.

Articulation with microphone technique. Adjust the vowels. The tongue tends to be flatter and more lateral than in traditional styles. You can be subtle with consonants in intimate styles and percussive in aggressive styles.

Tongue flexibility. Your tongue should be active. It does not need to be stationary behind the front teeth.

Stylistic embellishments. Include runs, slurs, cries, yodels, and other inflections, and achieve them with the breath and not with the throat.

Classical Singing Following Intensive Microphone Singing

Conversely, these are the problems I have dealt with and readjustments I have had to make when reverting to classical music following extensive work in microphone idioms:

- My sense of output vis-à-vis vocal effort is distorted (skewed) proprioceptively, since all the projection is achieved acoustically, with no electronic reinforcement from the microphone.
- I have to apportion my breath to achieve sustained breath control and energy when singing extended vocal lines as opposed to tailoring my phrasing to breath capacity.
- In high registers, I have the tendency to try and place the tones, to pinpoint pitches, resulting in vocal tension.
- Related to this, I feel that my intonation is not sufficiently exacting, particularly with the presence of a regular vibrato throughout the tone. I have the impression that vibrato may be excessive on

middle and high notes after practicing straight tone or using vibrato only at phrase endings in singing microphone styles.

- My tone focus may tend to be pinched with the palate not arched sufficiently in medium to high notes. Reorienting to head-voice resonance and the vocal qualities that ensue requires readjustment.

- My inability to hear myself through the monitors, particularly in acoustical performance venues with little reverberation, can be daunting. Being accustomed to monitoring from the sound speakers (which provides somewhat of a feedback loop and a level of assurance) entails significant adjustment initially. Research dealing with stuttering and the engagement of mirror neurons for fluency enhancement suggests that there may be some validity to this subjective response (Kalinowski and Saltuklaroglu 2003). For microphone singers, the absence of amplification may be disconcerting initially, resulting in insecurity.

- I reacquaint myself with pure vowels for projection, as well as prosody of foreign languages as opposed to vernacular English.

- I practice vocal pacing and conditioning, which are crucial to acquiring stamina for long and demanding programs.

ration continued to conform to the bel canto tradition until the emergence of rock and pop musicals, with popular/folk–styled roles, began to alter the vocal landscape, adding different sounds and stylistic approaches. Eventually, the introduction of head microphones, which modified vocal demands, coincided with increasingly amplified accompaniment with electronic synthesizers and prerecorded discs. This technology, when combined with sophisticated engineering, augmented the decibel level significantly, shifting vocal priorities. While the head mikes theoretically eased projection, the amplified accompaniment demanded increased output to match the reinforced pit orchestra. Whether a vocalist sings a patter tune or an intimate ballad or belts out a rock 'n' roll number, vocal preparation has to be adjusted to meet the new vocal demands of a changing professional performance environment.

As of the 1920s, beginning with the blues and "race records" (Pleasants 1974, 22) and continuing through the '30s and '40s with the movie musical and Big Band Era, singers were using the microphone at medium dynamic levels and crooning. Crooning emerged not strictly as an offshoot of the microphone and the classic blues but also in conjunction with studio technology, particularly recording for film. Judy, Fred, and Lena may have appeared to be breaking into song, but they were dubbed. Supersensitive microphones permitted singers to relax when they recorded these dubbed songs, assured that the sound would project even if the dynamic was barely above confidential speech.

Vocal coaches worked with unschooled, natural singers who usually sang convincingly enough and worked with the details of phrasing, diction, and stylistic inflection. When electric guitars and electric basses appeared, the dynamic levels required to keep the singers from being overpowered increased, and singing had to be more assertive. "An urban, electrified ensemble form of the blues" (Riedel 1972) emerged, which, when combined with electrified instruments, became known as rhythm and blues with its white counterpart labeled rock 'n' roll. The convergence of "all the musical currents of America's sub-cultures: black and white gospel, country and western (rockabilly) and rhythm and blues" (Pleasants 1974, 269) coalesced with the popularity of Elvis Presley. Their offshoots rock and soul (more derivative of black gospel) continued to influence singing styles, with emotional, forceful delivery, and morphed into hard rock, heavy metal, and other splinter styles. Projecting over electric guitars now feeding back and distorting necessitated loud, powerful, and aggressive vocal delivery to express anger, protest, and rebellion.

The visceral approach to singing and a vocal tone incorporating growls, cries, yodels, and other inflections were perceived as vulgar aesthetically and antithetical to artistic expression in academia, where, not unreasonably, the objective was beauty of tone. Glenn Basham, concertmaster of the Naples Symphony and professor of jazz and classical violin, says,

> Tone Quality: this is a tough one for classical musicians, because a typical "college trained" violinist spends thousands of hours (and dollars) finding that perfect, gorgeous, refined sound, and now she is being asked to toss that tone into Lake Osceola! or at least . . . to find other expressive means than simply vibrato, crescendo, and perfect intonation. The essence of the jazz language is that it is a vernacular tradition, English, but street English. Many classical musicians simply do not want to risk sounding unrefined, or when they try for the first time . . . it sounds so odd that they are afraid ever to try again. (Personal communication, July 8, 2005)

In idioms derivative of African American influences vocalists were self-taught and took advantage of opportunities to sing in church choirs and work with musical mentors. Eventually, vocal pedagogues who addressed commercial music styles operated in major cities independently of academia, serving more as coaches. Overtures into vocal production outside of the Western European bel canto tradition began in the late '70s and early '80s within the university setting but tended to focus on country and western, folk, and mainstream pop (avoiding microphone use and blues-derivative forms) and were approached primarily within the context of maintaining vocal health. The field of voice science, with the Voice Foundation and symposia devoted to care of the professional voice, examined vocal physiology and function, vocal disorders, and medical issues and investigated topics such as belting and vibrato within the context of experimental studies. Vocal health and hygiene issues became the motivation for pursuing pedagogy in the commercial fields. Concurrently, some recognition was accorded to alternative vocal approaches, especially contemporary classical compositions and the avant-garde, and jazz vocal programs emerged, principally within the context of show choir or jazz choirs.

By the late 1980s, professional opportunities as jingle singers and backup vocalists, as well as the merging of the recording industry with video technology, increased student demand for commercial music studies. By the end of the millennium, the National Association of Teachers of Singing's *Journal of Singing* was publishing articles devoted to advancing pedagogy in musical theatre as well as belting and alternative pedagogies. Nevertheless, in the 1990s, pedagogy exploring microphone idioms and blues-derivative singing along with the challenges posed by vocally adapting to R & B, soul, rap, and other aggressive styles in the ever-evolving commercial/jazz world was in the nascent stage. Meeting the needs of the contemporary vocalist performing in new genres and addressing performing situations constantly transformed by technology and a shrinking world will constitute a formidable and exciting challenge for vocal pedagogy well into the new millennium.

Pedagogical Adjustments to Musical Idioms

Classical (Traditional) Vocal Pedagogy

This includes opera, oratorio, art song (German, French, Italian, Spanish, Russian), and operetta. The pedagogical objectives are

- Development of the human voice as an acoustic, aerodynamic instrument capable of projecting over large instrumental ensembles and/or in large performance venues.
- Repertoire for vocal ranges from sustained legato to coloratura that demands flexibility and agility.
- Cultivation of the vocal range and color so that the voice projects acoustically to address music as written by composers in the literal music tradition.
- Classification of the individual instrument (soprano, tenor, baritone, bass, and subdivisions) to maximize its potential in terms of resonance, flexibility, and range, which dictates the body of literature the vocalist performs.
- Achievement of facility with foreign languages to communicate

text persuasively. In the words of Pierre Bernac, "In vocal music, the sonority and the rhythm of the words are an integral part of the music itself" (1978, 15).

- Instruction in tandem with musical accompaniment for a holistic musical treatment, a challenge in many settings. The vocal line should be united with musical accompaniment in ensemble to re-create the vision of the composer.

Musical Theatre

This includes roles in operetta and traditional musicals (Rodgers and Hammerstein, etc.), narrative ballads (Sondheim), cabaret, patter tunes, character tunes, rock musicals, and belting, as of this writing. The pedagogy involves

- Teaching toward musical roles and/or type. Some philosophies strive for versatility (for summer stock, theme parks, cruise ships).
- Seeking character voices and variety of vocal sounds.
- Working toward triple-threat singing, dancing, acting (Alt 2004).
- Integrating choreography and movement in vocal performance.
- Working with new musicals that constantly alter vocal landscape and musical demands.
- Using head microphones, which have slightly altered vocal approaches.
- Learning new technology that has altered instrumental accompaniment (electronic instruments, reduced live house band), thereby influencing vocal demands.

Commercial Music

This includes hillbilly, country, swing, blues, R & B, rock, soul, rap, standards, middle-of-the-road, power ballads, and ska, as of this writing. The pedagogy involves the following issues:

- Singers come in with a point of view regarding personal vocal sound, already singing, and imitating favorite artists.
- Students tend to display a practical approach to singing, seeking to solve vocal problems within the context of repertoire and in

performance mode. Teaching should seek to remove impediments toward effective vocal performance.

- Timbres sought tend to be represented by popular artists of the time, although increased diversity exists due to the iPod and other technology, individualizing musical exposure, tastes, and performance goals.
- The horizon is constantly changing, due to the ephemeral nature of artists and instrumentation. For example, in past decades, gospel influenced chest-voiced female artists; this style gave way to folk-like artists and then to coloratura-like divas. For the male voice, stratospheric tenor sounds were supplanted by full-voiced gravelly baritones at high registers, followed by declamatory rap artists with attitude in articulation and the contrasting breathy, light voices of boy bands.
- Instrumental tracks are constantly changing, from dance centered, to single piano or guitar, to synthesizers and sequencers, to individualized published disks with exotic synthetic and acoustical instruments.
- Vernacular English in the speaking range, with a constant infusion of new inflections and language and novel linguistic approaches, are constantly emerging.
- Students need to understand rhythmic nuances that are a part of many genres, including outer rhythm and stylistic subdivisions. They need to internalize musical grooves to enhance physical coordination.
- Teachers should appreciate if not enjoy stylistic subdivisions that convey attitude and a point of view that are implicit in the style.
- Teachers must convince students that optimal technique helps them achieve individuality in vocal timbres and the intensity they seek, along with sound vocal hygiene and maintenance.

Jazz

The subgenres include blues, swing, Latin (bossa nova, samba), acid jazz, funk, fusion, modal jazz, bebop, Afro-Cuban, salsa, and reggae. The pedagogical issues include the following:

- Like their classical counterparts, students are less likely to be familiar with history and tradition.

- Strong awareness of musical accompaniment is required, including knowledge of musical forms to facilitate interactions with the rhythm section, which does not just accompany but interacts with the soloist.
- The standard jazz repertoire, characterized by melodic, harmonic, and rhythmic sophistication, dictates high levels of musicianship to allow improvising and navigating complicated chord progressions, with extensions.
- Attention to vocal attacks and releases is important for rhythmic precision and energy.
- Improvisation and melodic variation sometimes supplant melodic material, but the original source of the melody should form a point of departure.
- Improvisation through scat singing entails achieving fluidity with scat syllables as well as theoretical knowledge of chord qualities, scales, modes, and rhythmic grooves.
- The choral jazz tradition, a subset of jazz, entails vocal and choral adjustments, including inhibiting vibrato to enable full complex chord sonorities with voices often separated by semitones.
- There can be a wide range of vocal approaches, including straight tone and vibrato at releases, as well as differing vocal styles dictated by rhythmic accompaniment, from duo to acoustic trio to big band to electrified blues, funk, and fusion.

Jazz Vocal Pedagogy

Perhaps we can define a jazz singer as someone who uses his or her instrument in a disciplined and intelligent manner to sing songs in a jazz setting and who, in a performance, will communicate not only a commitment to and love for the audience, but will also, at times, improvise within the framework of the music to create a performance that demonstrates a kind of premeditated spontaneity.

—Bruce Crowther and Mike Pinfold, *Singing Jazz:*
The Singers and Their Styles

Like their classical counterparts, aspiring jazz singers are less likely to be familiar with the history and tradition of jazz, not to mention the various schools, unless they were exposed to it courtesy of parents who are jazz aficionados. However, the demands on the jazz singer as a musician are more stringent because the true jazz vocalist improvises and reinvents on the spot, interacting with the spontaneity and inventiveness of the rhythm section, who are themselves responding to the vocalist. Therefore, being secure musically is of the utmost priority. Harmonic and rhythmic sophistication are integral to jazz, with improvised lines, melodic variation, and vocal embellishments developing out of original melodic material. Vocal improvisation through scat singing adds an additional dimension to jazz vocalism. Prominent jazz artists display a variety of vocal timbres, ranging from the breathy, sensuous Latin bossa nova to the R & B–flavored funk tune, in addition to revisiting swing, bebop, and torch ballads as part of the retro trend. Vocal jazz ensembles represent another subset of jazz singing, ranging from gospel-inflected groups to swinging quartets and university swing choirs and jazz vocal ensembles. Like any living, breathing vocal idiom, the sounds, rhythms, and styles are constantly dissected and transformed, requiring pedagogical approaches that are eclectic, addressing performance and musicianship within the individual subgenres while being mindful of the individual's vocal mechanism and stylistic orientation, which is (and should be) in a constant state of flux.

Jazz Singing

> In a nutshell, the bow is our breath, our lungs. . . . The attack of the first note of a phrase really must have some kind of articulation, stress, or gentle bite, as I call it. This sounds easy but is terribly hard for a classical player to actually do convincingly.
>
> —Glenn Basham, personal communication, July 8, 2005

The nature of musical genres dictates the application of the vocal instrument. In jazz, rhythm and time feel are central to authenticity, with concomitant influences on phrasing and inflection. Like commercial/popular styles, jazz can be categorized in terms of rhythmic underpinnings with subdivisions within the styles.

The aural–oral nature of jazz as opposed to the literal results in the development of a standard repertoire referred to conveniently as "standards" that encompasses these various rhythmic grooves. Jazzers make it their business to familiarize themselves melodically and harmonically with these standard tunes, using them as a point of departure for rein- terpretation and improvisation. The major broad categories include the traditional ballad, swing, bossa nova (and other Latin influences), jazz waltz, and funk/fusion.

In discussing crossing over instrumentally, the observations of instrumentalists are revealing and underscore the importance placed on rhythmic integrity. In the words of big band lead trumpeter O'Far- rill, "In jazz, precision or 'where things go' is more predictable and a priority. For an instrumentalist subbing on a gig, the challenges are rhythmic . . . trying to avoid playing in the space, with poor releases and time" (Chris O'Farrill, personal communication, December 13, 2005). Rhythmic figures, accentuated through attack and release, are integral to establishing a good swing feel particularly at brisk tempi. It is rhythmic consciousness that separates authentic jazz pedagogues with professional experience from classical pedagogues who may never have functioned professionally within the jazz idiom. While classical teach- ers may be able to appreciate and identify when a vocalist is swinging, they may not be able to identify the basic elements and mechanics emblematic of a genuine time feel, as can their instrumental colleagues. That is why interaction with jazz players represents the best teaching tool and why every opportunity to interact with instrumentalists should be exploited.

It is no coincidence that, though the majority of jazz singers were unschooled, vocalists who got experience through OJT (on-the-job training) while singing with big bands or small groups, on the gig, developed into vocal musicians. It is in pressure situations that funda- mental rhythmic and intuitive vocal sensibilities present themselves for all to hear. If exposure to live musicians is not readily available, practic- ing with tapes (Aebersold disks, etc.) can substitute for and supplement singing with live accompaniment.

In terms of phrasing and lyric interpretation, the singer needs to have achieved fluency with the words to such an extent that extempo- raneous interpretations are possible. Some respected jazz icons like Betty Carter take great liberties with phrasing, emphasizing rhythmic figures at the expense of the lyrics, a stylistic choice viewed critically by some. Others (Peggy Lee and Shirley Horn) deliver the lyric in a style more closely aligned to modal speech and almost devoid of sustained phonation yet manage to effectively communicate a variety of subtle shades of emotion.

Listening to artists' renditions and imitating them can help inspire a novice vocalist initially but also inhibit individualized interpretation in the long run. Ultimately, unlike the instrumentalists who present song material in the abstract, without words, singers communicate a song and vibe with specific lyrics and emotion embodied in the text. Hence, their take on the poetry needs to be implied in their vocal delivery.

Surrendering to the time feel set by the accompaniment and becoming part of the groove automatically produce some aspects of the vocal quality and phrasing demanded. For example, the close alliance of text and time feel is highlighted when a singer moves from a mellow bossa nova to a hard, up-tempo swing because the vocal quality, reflecting the contrasting mood, changes abruptly. In the bossa, the timbres from the band are somewhat muted, with the vocals more breathy and intimate, almost straight-tone. In more up-tempo songs, the driving swing of the band is complemented by an edgy, emphatic vocal delivery.

The attack into the first note of a phrase (called articulations by jazz arrangers) becomes particularly important for the jazz vocalist. It also has implications for vocal flexibility and agility, particularly in scatting and when projecting over brass and large ensembles. Therefore issues of coordinated attack (onset) and correct pronunciation of initial consonants merit special attention, particularly for the R & B–flavored jazz styles.

While a jazz singer may tend to gravitate toward a particular jazz substyle (Latin, swing, funk, blues, modal, retro, etc.), musical growth is ever-evolving—an exploration of new vocal timbres and rhythms. Ultimately, the energy and rhythmic conviction of the band is the direct responsibility of the soloist who is fronting the band. If instrumentalists are aware that the vocalist is listening and aware of chord changes and subtle alterations in time feel and appreciates tasty voicings or drum fills, the band will contribute enthusiastically toward achieving highly creative performance levels.

Jazz Improvisation

It is no coincidence that, with a few exceptions, most scat singers were originally instrumentalists. Not infrequently, you can see them mentally playing as their fingers move on their invisible instrument as they scat. Vocal improvisation in the form of scat singing is particularly challenging because it enlists different areas of the brain and cognition. Scat syllables and rhythms essentially function like a new articulatory language with its own syntax, while music processing is generally associated with right-brain function. Therefore two distinct tasks are represented in jazz improvisation. Achieving fluidity in articulation and maintaining a comfortable time feel while also negotiating chord changes is a formidable task.

Instrumentalists have the advantage of tactile memory through practice and internalization of chord scales and the muscle memory of fingering. While many may claim to prehear the notes and phrases, mechanical proprioception nonetheless provides valuable assistance, particularly with valved and pitched instruments. Vocalists, on the other hand, must decidedly perceive a pitch in advance to sing in tune while also employing new articulatory patterns. However, improvisation is a high-order musical experience and a richly rewarding one. For the singer exploring improvisation and scat singing, here are some strategies as well as valuable resources:

- Listen to great scat solos and do an oral transcription, essentially imitating the model. As you become comfortable through repetition, you should be able to perform a solo persuasively, sounding spontaneous, as if it was your own conception.
- Make it a point to recognize harmonic patterns and learn chord changes to tunes, particularly standards.
- Literally transcribe favorite scat solos in order to recognize rhythmic and melodic patterns as well as the development of themes and ideas.
- Listen to instrumental solos for rhythmic patterns, phrasing, inflections, and development of solos, among other elements.
- Practice with prerecorded tracks such as those by Jamey Aebersold and *Choice Standards* by Sher Music Company.

- Write a vocalese, writing lyrics to famous instrumental solos. The skill comes with developing the rhythm, intonation, and stress of the language to respond to the rhythm, accents, and melodic contour of the music. Jon Hendricks of Lambert, Hendricks, and Ross provides a number of excellent examples, such as Manhattan Transfer's "Until I Met You."
- Conversely, begin with the text as a point of departure in creating a solo. The rhythm of the language will generate rhythmic and melodic lines which will help you develop a personalized attitude and inflection.
- Isolate the rhythmic elements from the melodic elements. Practice scat syllables and figures with a metronome to become comfortable maintaining fluidity while swinging.
- For melodic material, use the melody as a point of departure initially. When asked what inspired him, Jon Hendricks replied that he used the melody as a source of improv, a strong endorsement for that approach. It can (1) prevent generic improvisation over standard chord sequences, which can tend to sound like exercises rather than incorporating the individual tune's unique qualities and mood, and (2) present a font of fertile melodic ideas (retrograde, developing fragments of the melody for motives, contouring at a higher or lower tonal level, to name a few) for a solo.
- Strive to sculpt a solo, working from simple to complex, using dynamic contrast from soft to loud, and building room to expand and explore lower range to upper range, with peaks and valleys.
- Music is time and space. Don't be afraid of pauses for listening and responding to the music from the instrumentalists around you. Come up for air.
- Rehearse in real time out loud so that you can become comfortable hearing yourself. Don't mentally fast-forward or use a series of starts and stops to regroup, since you do not have that option in performance.
- Practice a solo repeatedly, which will generate patterns and ideas, allowing you to acquire vocabulary. Instrumentalists do so, preparing ideas and stocking away licks and rhythmic ideas.
- Have a mental outline (derived from a sketched outline or not) that will provide you with a measure of assurance and help you

avoid running dry in the pressure of performance. It merely serves as a blueprint, something you can hold on to, as a point of departure from which you can deviate, responding to what the rhythm section feeds you and what you come up with in the moment. The combination of extemporization and familiarity brought about by practicing can coalesce into a confident, creative, and satisfying solo.

Teaching the Versatile Vocalist in Academe

To satisfy the increasing demand for real-world competencies for the millennium, vocal departments might have the following characteristics:

- They are staffed not only with university-degreed teachers but with empirically trained singers—that is, performers who have learned by doing, who have been successful within the music industry, and whose success attests the fact that they have achieved some insight into what it takes. They may not possess degrees but have commensurate experience and could be considered artists in residence. They need not always be adjunct faculty.
- They offer vocal health and hygiene as an integral part of voice teaching in all idioms. Projection over walls of electronic sound and high-efficiency phonation such as belting demand a great deal of knowledge and skill from a vocalist. Arming singers with the knowledge of good vocal hygiene and maintenance awards them a measure of control over their instrument. It also better equips them to explore vocally demanding idioms in which artists have managed to display some measure of longevity. (A working relationship with a certified speech pathologist and an otolaryngologist sensitive to singers' needs to whom students can be referred is indispensable.)
- They offer opportunities for voice lessons in many styles and idioms. The assumption has always been that classical technique forms the foundation for all singing; however, in the last few years consistent evidence has emerged that, conversely, acquiring a good technique and facility for singing in a variety of idioms and

throughout the range (speech range, middle, and upper registers) permits the singer to perform classical pieces quite successfully. I have had a number of students who, upon being able to sing comfortably and authentically within the jazz/commercial idioms, decided to explore classical repertoire as well and did so with much enthusiasm! Ultimately, in a roundabout way, becoming the complete vocalist is not an impossible goal.

- They maintain flexible admission standards. It is not uncommon for mature singers who have experienced success as professional performers, having learned on the job, to decide to pursue a degree to refine their musical skills (particularly reading), or quite simply to learn more about their art form. Their inability to render a classical audition should not disqualify them. Ironically, the university can eventually serve as a real cultural center—a mecca that permits artists to explore and perform material within musical genres that, by their complex and esoteric nature, would not be heard otherwise nor be appreciated by a wide audience.

- They maintain relationships with leaders in the industry, as well as recent graduates and alumnae, to get feedback regarding any gaps that might exist in students' musical preparation. Pedagogues within the jazz/commercial idioms must constantly update, staying attuned to emerging musical styles, trends, and technology as well as the competencies that jingle and/or record producers and other industry leaders are demanding.

- They coordinate with departments of speech/language pathology as well as theatre arts departments, speech divisions, or schools of communication, which can provide a coordinated, interdisciplinary approach to vocalism, representing differing perspectives and transcending boundaries in vocal expression. This also encourages a kind of cross-pollination with related disciplines, which could apply in a variety of professional areas, benefit and broaden the background of students who are professional voice users, and improve aural communication.

Vocal performance departments need to

- Address music education: Prepare teachers to tune in to what children are listening and relating to so that they stay current;

this could include rap, rock, hip-hop, and Latin rhythms, particularly in view of the changing demographics of American schoolchildren.

- Address the musical and vocal needs of composition-oriented singers, who may write, record, and produce their own material.
- Address jazz, including improvisation, which incorporates an advanced level of musicianship.
- Accommodate adult student and continuing education populations that will have diverse backgrounds and competencies to contribute to the academic environment.
- Augment the musicianship level of vocalists to increase the number of singers capable of performing contemporary classical compositions.
- Integrate technological advances in keyboard accompaniment as well as recording and video technology to facilitate instrumental accompaniment and pedagogical observation.
- Explore world music in conjunction with ethnomusicology and sociology to incorporate universal perspectives in music.
- Serve as eclectic music centers operating independently of commercial constraints so they can present music of artistic value that, due to its esoteric nature, will generate limited audiences.

Future Directions

In absorbing musical influences from around the world, singers will be exploring quarter-tone scales and a variety of vocal approaches that can teach them to be adaptable and to use the vocal mechanism in broad, sustained lines as well as flexible, articulated musical expression. Ultimately, a student's career may turn in any direction, but the ability to sing in a variety of idioms and settings leaves vocalists better equipped to make music a part of their work as well as their play—the dream of every one of our students.

Tips for Listening

Listen

- To the big picture, the textures and rhythmic feel of instrumental accompaniment, as well as the small picture, the vocal soloist. Don't focus on only one element or one instrument.
- To how the elements interact and coalesce to become an ensemble.
- To imitation in thematic material, rhythmic pattern, or timbres that suggest that everyone is listening and reacting to each other.
- To how the outer rhythm is generated and how attention is given, however subtle, to the rhythmic pulse as well.
- To a vocalist at different stages in his/her career (early, middle, later) as well as with varying instrumental backup. Most singers evolve, and some fade away; it's best not to draw conclusions on a brief sampling of one phase. For example, note the transformation of Joni Mitchell's voice from the clear, smooth (no breaks) sounds of the folk tune "Chelsea Morning" to the deeper, heavier vocal timbre deliberately developed in later years to sing jazz in *Mingus*.
- To become aware of those sidemen on recordings who distinguish themselves as musical influences and occasionally mentors. Their presence at a recording or on stage is a barometer of respect for the vocalist.
- To vocalists performing in different instrumental settings to note any changes or accommodation to strings, and so on. Hearing

them live or recorded in different venues or situations offers interesting opportunities for comparison. For example, Shirley Horn has some cuts that are self-accompanied, some with rhythm section, and others with lush string arrangements. Most artists have performed in at least two different instrumental scenarios. Compare their vocal approaches and musical choices.

- To each vocalist and group with an open mind. A vocalist distinguished enough to qualify for a listen has something special or unique to offer that has enabled him or her to endure.

Some suggestions for singer–songwriters:

- Joni Mitchell
- Tom Lehrer
- B. B. King
- Raul Midon
- Michael Tomlinson
- Stevie Wonder

Some suggestions for duos:

- Tuck and Patty
- Norma Winstone and John (Jazz) Taylor
- Jackie and Roy
- Chick Corea and Bobby McFerrin
- Tony Bennett and Bill Evans
- Nancy Marano and Eddie Montiero
- Nancy Wilson and George Shearing

Suggestions for singers with a rhythm section:

- Nat King Cole
- Nancy Wilson
- Ella Fitzgerald
- Mel Tormé
- Joe Williams
- Cleo Lane

- Sarah Vaughan
- Mark Murphy
- Shirley Horn
- Dinah Washington
- Betty Carter
- Eddy Jefferson
- Chet Baker
- Johnny Hartman

Some emerging artists worthy of note:

- Kurt Elling
- Dianne Reeves
- Tierney Sutton
- Claudia Acuna
- Ernestine Anderson
- Roseanna Vitro
- Dee Dee Bridgewater
- Carmen Lundy
- Kevin Mahogany

Suggestions for singers with orchestras:

- Barbara Streisand
- Nancy King
- Dawn Upshaw
- Linda Eder
- Maureen McGovern
- Audra McDonald
- Kristin Chenoweth

Suggestions for singers with big bands:

- Frank Sinatra
- Billie Holiday
- Ella Fitzgerald
- Anita O'Day

- Mel Tormé
- Patti Austen
- Dianne Schurr
- Maureen McGovern
- Kevin Mahogany
- Natalie Cole
- Nancy Marano

And some for rock and blues:

- Al Jarreau
- George Benson
- Kenny Loggins
- Michael McDonald
- Anne Wilson
- Bobby Caldwell
- Aaron Neville
- Sting
- Linda Ronstadt
- The Bee Gees
- Jon Secada
- Aretha Franklin
- Gladys Knight
- Alanis Morrisette

Who's Who

- **Glenn Basham** is the concertmaster of the Naples Philharmonic, a member of the Bergonzi String Quartet, and a jazz violinist and professor at the University of Miami.
- **Gary Keller** is a symphonic and jazz saxophonist and professor of jazz saxophone at the University of Miami. His CD *Blues for an Old New Age* and those he recorded as a member of the Miami Saxophone Quartet have received critical acclaim.
- **Larry Lapin** is known internationally as an arranger, composer, pianist, and teacher. He is the program director of the Studio Music and Jazz Program at the University of Miami and the director of the award-winning jazz vocal ensemble JV1.
- **Sheila Marchant Barish** has sung musical theatre roles and classical literature and for conferences devoted to new age music and philosophy. She has taught college voice as well as having a successful private studio for over twenty-five years, with students who are recording artists, on cruise ships, and in musical theatre.
- **Raul Midon** is a recording artist (*State of Mind*) who has garnered critical and audience acclaim as a vocalist–guitarist who transcends stylistic boundaries. He has also done work extensively as a studio singer.
- **Bruce Miller**, award-winning teacher and director, is the director of acting programs at the University of Miami and the author of two books, *The Actor as Storyteller* and *Head-First Acting*, and numerous articles in *Dramatics* magazine and *Teaching Theatre*.

- **Chris O'Farrill** is an orchestral classical trumpeter and lead trumpet for a number of jazz big bands including those of Woody Herman and Milton Mustafa. He is also a writer and arranger.
- **Alexander Pope Norris** has been one of the leading studio trumpet players in New York City for many years.
- **Wendy Pederson** has been an active studio, blues, and jazz singer for over twenty years. The slate of artists she has performed with includes Julio and Enrique Iglesias, Jennifer Lopez, James Brown, and Gloria Estefan, to name a few.
- **Jon Secada** is a Grammy Award–winning artist and composer who has sung Latin pop and jazz and on Broadway. He holds a master's degree from the University of Miami and has taught voice at the college level.
- **Julie Silvera-Jensen** is a professional award-winning jazz vocalist and teacher with a DMA in jazz vocal performance.
- **Janos Starker** is an internationally renowned cellist and teacher and is the author of the memoir *The World of Music According to Starker*.

References

Alt, David. "Triple Threat Training Program's Weakest Area—Reading Music: Reinforcing Sight Reading in the Voice Studio for Singer/Actors." *Journal of Singing* 60, no. 4 (2004): 389–393.

Barrett, Richard. "A Century of Microphones: The Implications of Amplification for the Singer and the Listener." *Journal of Singing* 61, no. 3 (2005): 273–277.

Bernac, Pierre. *The Interpretation of French Song.* New York: W. W. Norton & Company, 1978.

Brady, James. "In Step with Kristin Chenoweth." *Parade* (May 15, 2005): 16.

Buescher, Randy. "Popular Song and Musical Theater: The Recovering Female Opera Singer." *Journal of Singing* 61, no. 5 (2005): 517–519.

Charlton, Katherine. *Rock Music Styles: A History.* Dubuque, IA: Wm. C. Brown Publishers, 1990.

Cooper, Gloria. "Once More with Feeling: The Crossover Artist's First Step in Making an Emotional Connection with a Popular or Jazz Song." *Journal of Singing* 60, no. 2 (2003): 153–157.

Crowther, Bruce, and Mike Pinfold. *Singing Jazz: The Singers and Their Styles.* San Francisco: Miller Freeman Books, 1997.

Eisenson, Jon. *Voice and Diction: A Program for Improvement,* 5th ed. New York: Macmillan, 1985.

Gillett, Charlie. *The Sound of the City.* New York: Outerbridge and Diensffrey, 1970.

Greene, Margaret C. L., and L. Mathieson. *The Voice and Its Disorders,* 5th ed. San Diego, CA: Singular Publishing Group, 1989.

Kalinowski, J., and T. Saltuklaroglu. "Speaking with a Mirror: Engagement of Mirror Neurons via Choral Speech and Its Derivatives Induces Stuttering Inhibition." *Medical Hypotheses* 60 (2003): 538–543.

Lapin, Lawrence. "The Elements of Jazz Vocal Performance." Handout from the IAJE Teacher Training Institute, Atlanta, GA, June 2004.

Lebon, Rachel L. "The Development and Evaluation of a Guide to Teach Selected Elements of Commercial Singing." Masters Abstracts International, 1980.

———. "Vocal Pedagogy within Jazz/Commercial Idioms." Paper presented at the annual meeting of the National Association of Schools of Music, Boston, November 1998.

———. The Professional Vocalist: A Handbook for Commercial Singers and Teachers. Lanham, MD: Scarecrow Press, 1999.

LoVetri, Jeannette. "Vocal Pedagogy: Female Chest Voice." Journal of Singing 60, no. 2 (2003): 161–164.

Miller, Bruce. "The Audition: Putting the Song Across." Dramatics (September 1999).

Miller, Richard. English, French, German, and Italian Techniques of Singing Revisited. Lanham, MD: Scarecrow Press, 1997.

———. The Structure of Singing. New York: Schirmer, 1986.

Montagne, Renée, and Ashley Kahn. "Raul Midon: State of Mind." All Things Considered, National Public Radio, June 10, 2005.

Plant, Lourin. "Singing African-American Spirituals: A Reflection on Racial Barriers in Classical Vocal Music." Journal of Singing 61, no. 5 (2005): 451.

Pleasants, Henry. The Great American Popular Singers. New York: Simon and Schuster, 1974.

Riedel, Johannes. Soul Music: Black and White. Minneapolis, MN: Augsburg Publishing House, 1972.

Sable, Barbara Kinsey. "The Lilt of Language." NATS Journal 47, no. 5 (1991): 10–13.

Sidran, Ben. Black Talk. New York: Da Capo Press, 1971.

Spradling, Diana R. "Vocal Jazz and Its Credibility in the University Curriculum." Jazz Educators Journal 32, no. 5 (2000).

Stamberg, Susan. "Janos Starker: A Cellist's Memoir." Morning Edition, National Public Radio, November 11, 2004.

Stearns, Marshall. The Story of Jazz. New York: Mentor, 1958.

Steinhous-Jordan, Barbara. "Black Spiritual Art Song: Interpretive Guidelines for Studio Teachers." Journal of Singing 61, no. 5 (2005): 482.

Sundberg, Johann. The Science of the Singing Voice. DeKalb: Northern Illinois University Press, 1987.

Tini, April Arabian, and Dennis Tini. "The Vocal/Piano Jazz Duo." Clinic presented at the 21st Annual Convention for the International Association of Jazz Educators (IAJE), Boston, January 1994.

Titze, Ingo, et al. "Voice Research and Technology: Laryngeal Muscle Activity in a Tonal Scale: Comparing Speech-like to Song-like Productions in a Mezzo-soprano." *Journal of Singing* 59, no. 1 (2002): 49–56.

Vennard, William. *Singing: The Mechanism and Technic*. New York: Carl Fischer, 1967.

Vitro, Roseanna. "Vocalists Are from Venus: Instrumentalists Are from Mars: Skills in Communication between Vocal and Instrumental Musicians." Paper presented at the annual convention of the International Association of Jazz Educators, Atlanta, GA, January 1996.

Weir, Michele. *Jazz Singers Handbook*. Van Nuys, CA: Alfred Publication Co., 2005.

Zemlin, Willard R. *Speech and Hearing Science*, 2d ed. Englewood Cliffs, NJ: Prentice-Hall, 1981.

Index

About the Author

Rachel L. Lebon has sung all over the world, including a State Department tour of the former Soviet Union and Portugal as well as a tour with the U.S. Air Force Tops in Blues, during which she performed for troops throughout the United States, Alaska, Hawaii, and the Aleutian Islands and in Southeast Asia. She has done extensive club and studio work, as well as some network television work in the Dallas Fort Worth Metroplex, in Nashville, and throughout Florida. Within the concert realm she has performed concerts with jazz bands and concert bands and has also done oratorio work, including premiers of works by contemporary composers. Her jazz CD, *Voicings*, was released in 2004. She holds bachelor's and master's degrees from the University of North Texas (formerly North Texas State University) and a Ph.D. from the University of Miami. Her teaching experience includes classical and commercial singing at Belmont College, musical theatre within the Department of Theatre Arts, and classical voice at the University of Miami, where she is professor and coordinator of jazz voice. She is a member of the Professional Voice Institute, an interdisciplinary team devoted to the treatment of voice disorders and is an active clinician worldwide. The author of *The Professional Vocalist: A Handbook for Commercial Singers and Teachers*, she has also published articles in the *Journal of the National Association of Teachers of Singing*. Dr. Lebon continues to take pride in the accomplishments of her students who are recording, teaching, and sharing their musical perspective and talent throughout the world.